PRENTICE HALL

MIDDLE GRADES MATH
TOOLS FOR SUCCESS

COURSE 3

Practice Workbook

ISBN 0-13-435422-2

Printed in the United States of America.
 2 3 4 5 6 7 8   03 02 01 00 99 98

Editorial Services: Visual Education Corporation

Table of Contents

Answers to Practice Worksheets appear in the Teacher's Edition and in the back of each Chapter Support File.

Chapter 1

Practice 1-1 1
Practice 1-2 2
Practice 1-3 3
Practice 1-4 4
Practice 1-5 5
Practice 1-6 6
Practice 1-7 7
Practice 1-8 8
Practice 1-9 9
Practice 1-10 10
Practice 1-11 11

Chapter 2

Practice 2-1 12
Practice 2-2 13
Practice 2-3 14
Practice 2-4 15
Practice 2-5 16
Practice 2-6 17
Practice 2-7 18
Practice 2-8 19
Practice 2-9 20
Practice 2-10 21
Practice 2-11 22

Chapter 3

Practice 3-1 23
Practice 3-2 24
Practice 3-3 25
Practice 3-4 26
Practice 3-5 27
Practice 3-6 28
Practice 3-7 29
Practice 3-8 30
Practice 3-9 31
Practice 3-10 32

Chapter 4

Practice 4-1 33
Practice 4-2 34
Practice 4-3 35

Practice 4-4 36
Practice 4-5 37
Practice 4-6 38
Practice 4-7 39
Practice 4-8 40
Practice 4-9 41
Practice 4-10 42

Chapter 5

Practice 5-1 43
Practice 5-2 44
Practice 5-3 45
Practice 5-4 46
Practice 5-5 47
Practice 5-6 48
Practice 5-7 49
Practice 5-8 50
Practice 5-9 51
Practice 5-10 52

Chapter 6

Practice 6-1 53
Practice 6-2 54
Practice 6-3 55
Practice 6-4 56
Practice 6-5 57
Practice 6-6 58
Practice 6-7 59
Practice 6-8 60
Practice 6-9 61
Practice 6-10 62

Chapter 7

Practice 7-1 63
Practice 7-2 64
Practice 7-3 65
Practice 7-4 66
Practice 7-5 67
Practice 7-6 68
Practice 7-7 69
Practice 7-8 70
Practice 7-9 71

Chapter 8

Practice 8-1 72
Practice 8-2 73
Practice 8-3 74
Practice 8-4 75
Practice 8-5 76
Practice 8-6 77
Practice 8-7 78
Practice 8-8 79
Practice 8-9 80
Practice 8-10 81

Chapter 9

Practice 9-1 82
Practice 9-2 83
Practice 9-3 84
Practice 9-4 85
Practice 9-5 86
Practice 9-6 87
Practice 9-7 88
Practice 9-8 89
Practice 9-9 90
Practice 9-10 91

Chapter 10

Practice 10-1 92
Practice 10-2 93
Practice 10-3 94
Practice 10-4 95
Practice 10-5. 96
Practice 10-6 97
Practice 10-7 98
Practice 10-8 99
Practice 10-9 100
Practice 10-10 101
Practice 10-11 102

Chapter 11

Practice 11-1 103
Practice 11-2 104
Practice 11-3 105
Practice 11-4 106
Practice 11-5. 107
Practice 11-6 108
Practice 11-7 109
Practice 11-8 110

Enrichment/Minds on Math

1-1 through 1-3 111
1-4 through 1-7 112
1-8 through 1-11 113
2-1 through 2-3 114
2-4 through 2-7 115
2-8 through 2-11 116
3-1 through 3-3 117
3-4 through 3-6 118
3-7 through 3-10 119
4-1 through 4-3 120
4-4 through 4-6 121
4-7 through 4-10 122
5-1 through 5-3 123
5-4 through 5-6 124
5-7 through 5-10 125
6-1 through 6-3 126
6-4 through 6-6 127
6-7 through 6-10 128
7-1 through 7-3 129
7-4 through 7-6 130
7-7 through 7-9 131
8-1 through 8-3 132
8-4 through 8-6 133
8-7 through 8-10 134
9-1 through 9-3 135
9-4 through 9-6 136
9-7 through 9-10 137
10-1 through 10-3 138
10-4 through 10-7 139
10-8 through 10-11 140
11-1 through 11-3 141
11-4 through 11-6 142
11-7 through 11-8 143

Practice 1-1 *Organizing and Displaying Data*

Use this TV viewing data for Exercises 1–4.

Average Viewing Time 8:00 P.M.–11:00 P.M. (Mon.–Sun.)		
Age Group	Male	Female
18–24	6 h 40 min	7 h 42 min
25–54	9 h 23 min	10 h 3 min
55+	12 h 19 min	13 h 7 min

Source: *Nielson Media Research*

1. Make a sliding bar graph where each bar represents an age group.

2. Make a double bar graph.

3. In which graph is it easier to compare the viewing times within each age group? _____

4. In which graph is it easier to compare the viewing times within each gender? _____

Use data from this table for Exercises 5–7.

Population (100,000s)		
Year	Hialeah, FL	Birmingham, AL
1950	0.2	3.3
1960	0.7	3.4
1970	1.0	3.0
1980	1.5	2.8
1990	1.9	2.7

Source: *U.S. Bureau of the Census*

5. Make a stacked bar graph. Let each bar represent a year.

6. Make a multiple line graph.

7. In which graph is it easier to see which city's population has increased the most? _____

Practice 1-2 Reading Graphs Critically

Use the graph at the right for Exercises 1–4.

1. Which age group appears to have about nine times as many people as the number of people in the 15–24 age group?

   _____

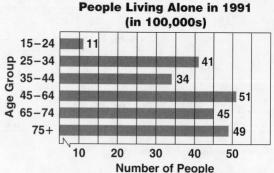

People Living Alone in 1991 (in 100,000s)

Age Group — Number of People

- 15–24: 11
- 25–34: 41
- 35–44: 34
- 45–64: 51
- 65–74: 45
- 75+: 49

Source: *U.S. Bureau of the Census*

2. Which age group actually has about five times as many people living alone as the 15–24 age group?

   _____

3. Draw a new bar graph to give an accurate impression of the data.

4. Explain why you chose to draw the graph as you have.

   _____

   _____

5. Use the data below to draw a graph that exaggerates the popularity of all-time favorite TV shows.

Show	Households Watching (100,000s)
*M*A*S*H*	50
Dallas	41
Roots Part VIII	36
Super Bowl XVI	40

Source: *A.C. Nielson estimates.*

6. Draw a graph that gives an accurate impression of the data.

7. Explain why you chose to draw the graph as you have.

   _____

8. Give a reason someone might draw a graph of the information that is misleading. _____

   _____

Practice 1-3 Displaying Frequency

Use the Olympic medal data at the right for Exercises 1–3.

1. Make a frequency table.
   Do not use intervals.

1992 Winter Olympics Silver Medals	
Country	**Medals**
Germany	10
Austria	7
Unified Team	6
Norway	6
Italy	6
France	5
United States	4
Canada	3
China	3
Japan	2
Luxembourg	2
Finland	1
Netherlands	1
South Korea	1
New Zealand	1

Source: *World Almanac and Book of Facts*

2. Draw a line plot.

3. Draw a histogram.

Use these ages of bike club members for Exercises 4 and 5.

19 16 10 14 15 19 13 14 15 16 21 14 12 14 16 13 13

4. Using intervals, display the data in a frequency table.

5. Use the frequency table to draw a histogram.

Practice 1-4 Measures of Central Tendency

Choose a calculator, pencil and paper, or mental math.
Find the mean, median, and mode of each of the following.

1. hours of piano practice

   _____

   Hours Mr. Capelli's students practice

   2 1 2 0 1 2 2 1 2 2

2. days of snow per month

   _____

   Monthly snow days in Central City

   8 10 5 1 0 0 0 0 0 1 3 12

3. number of students per class

   _____

   Class size in Westmont Middle School

   32 26 30 35 25 24 35 30 29 25

4. ratings given by students to a new movie

   _____

   Student ratings of a movie

   10 9 10 8 9 7 5 3 8 9 9 10 9 9 7

5. points scored in five basketball games

   _____

   Points scored by Westmont JV

   72 67 83 92 54

6. bowling scores for one bowler

   _____

   Li's bowling scores

   129 136 201 146 154

What is the best measure of central tendency for each type
of data—mean, median, or mode? Explain.

7. most popular movie in the past month

   _____

   _____

8. favorite hobby

   _____

   _____

9. class size in a school

   _____

   _____

10. ages of members in a club

    _____

    _____

Each person has taken four tests and has one more test to
take. Find the score that each person must make to change
the mean or median as shown.

11. Barry has scores of 93, 84, 86, and 75.
    He wants to raise the mean to 86.

    _____

12. Liz has scores of 87, 75, 82, and 93.
    She wants to raise the median to 87.

    _____

13. Jim has scores of 60, 73, 82, and 75.
    He wants to raise the mean to 75.

    _____

14. Andrea has scores of 84, 73, 92, and 88.
    She wants the median to be 86.

    _____

Practice 1-5 *Stem-and-Leaf Plots*

The stem-and-leaf plot at the right shows
the bowling scores for 20 bowlers.
Use the plot for Exercises 1–3.

10	0 2 2 4 4 4
11	1 3 5 5 5 9
12	4 5 9 9
13	0 6 8 8

13 | 8 means 138

1. What numbers make up the stems?

_____

2. What are the leaves for the stem 12?

_____

3. Find the median, mode, and range.

_____

Make a stem-and-leaf plot for each set of data. Then find
the median, mode, and range.

4. 8 19 27 36 35 24 6 15 16 24 38 23 20

_____

5. 8.6 9.1 7.4 6.3 8.2 9.0 7.5 7.9 6.3 8.1 7.1 8.2 7.0 9.6 9.9

_____

6. 436 521 470 586 692 634 417 675 526 719 817

_____

7. 17.9 20.4 18.6 19.5 17.6 18.5 17.4 18.5 19.4

_____

The back-to-back stem-and-leaf plot at
the right shows the high and low
temperatures for a week in a certain
city. Use this plot for Exercises 8–10.

Low		High
8 7	5	
4 3	6	5 9 9
2 1 0	7	2 5 6
	8	0

63 ← 3 | 6 | 2 → 62

8. Find the range for the high temperatures.

_____

9. Find the median for the low temperatures.

_____

10. Find the mode for the high temperatures.

_____

11. Make a back-to-back stem-and-leaf plot for the following data.
Find the median and mode for each set of data.

Set A: 75 82 79 80 75 76 83 74 75 86 80 71 75 _____

Set B: 71 73 75 80 79 80 74 80 74 79 76 80 81 _____

Course 3 Chapter 1

Practice 1-6 Box-and-Whisker Plots

Use the box-and-whisker plot below to find each of the following.

Height in Inches

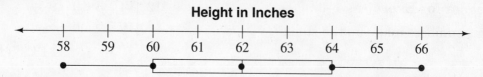

1. the median height _____
2. the lower quartile _____
3. the upper quartile _____
4. the greatest height _____
5. the shortest height _____
6. the range of heights _____

Make a box-and-whisker plot for each set of data.

7. 8 10 11 7 12 6 10 5 9 7 10

8. 20 21 25 18 25 15 27 26 24 23 20 20

9.

Cargo Airlines in the U.S. (1991)	
Airline	Freight ton-miles (1,000,000s)
Federal Express	3,622
Northwest	1,684
United	1,214
American	884
Delta	668
Continental	564
Pan American	377
Trans World	369
United Parcel Service	210

Source: *Air Transport Association of America*

10.

Immigration to the U.S. (1981–1990)	
Country	Number (1,000s)
Mexico	1,656
Philippines	549
China	347
Korea	334
Vietnam	281
Dominican Republic	252
India	251
El Salvador	214
Jamaica	208
United Kingdom	159

Source: *U.S. Dept. of Justice*

Practice 1-7 Making Predictions from Scatter Plots

Tell whether a scatter plot made for each set of data would show a positive trend, a negative trend, or no trend.

1. amount of education and annual salary

   _____

2. weight and speed in a foot race

   _____

3. test score and shoe size

   _____

For the scatter plots in Exercises 4 and 5, use a computer or graph the points by hand.

4. Make a scatter plot showing the number of homeowners on one axis and vacation homeowners on the other axis. If there is a trend, draw a trend line.

Residents of Maintown

Year	Homeowners	Vacation Homeowners
1997–98	2,050	973
1996–97	1,987	967
1995–96	1,948	1,041
1994–95	1,897	1,043
1993–94	1,862	1,125
1992–93	1,832	1,126

5. Draw the data in a scatter plot. If there is a trend, draw a trend line.

Studying Time vs. Number of Correct Words

Time Spent Studying (minutes)	Number of Words Spelled Correctly
40	20
35	18
32	16
30	16
20	15
15	15
10	10
10	8

6. Wynetta found the graph shown at the right. The title of the graph was missing. What could the graph be describing?

   _____

   _____

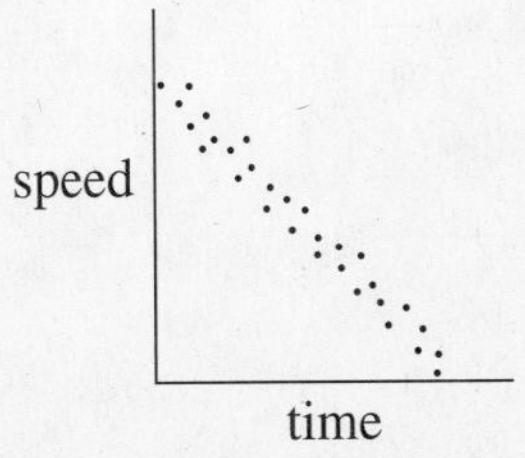

Practice 1-8 Choosing an Appropriate Graph

Use the circle graph.

Where Americans Buy Used Cars

1. From which group are about $\frac{1}{3}$ of used cars purchased?

   _____

2. If 49,778 people bought used cars one month, estimate how many bought them from a dealership.

   _____

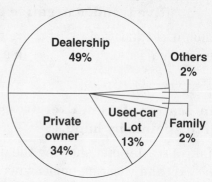

Source: *USA Today from Ameripoll, Maritz Marketing Research*

Decide which of the two types of graphs is an appropriate display for the given data. Explain your choice.

3. line graph or circle graph?
   sizes of U.S. farms from 1950 to 1990

   _____

4. bar graph or scatter plot?
   lengths of rivers

   _____

5. scatter plot or histogram?
   height versus weight of students in a class

   _____

6. scatter plot or circle graph?
   the way a family budgets its income

   _____

Decide which of the two types of graphs is an appropriate display for the given data. Then, make the graph.

7. bar graph or line graph?

   _____

U.S. Endangered Animals as of 1992	
Type of Animal	**Number of Endangered Species**
Mammals	305
Birds	226
Reptiles	80
Amphibians	14
Fish	66
Snails	8
Crustaceans	8
Insects	14
Arachnids	3

Source: *U.S. Fish and Wildlife Service*

Practice 1-9 *Conducting a Survey*

In a mall, 2,146 shoppers (age 16 and older) were asked, "How often do you buy shoe polish?" Here is how they responded.

1. What population does the sample represent?

   _____

   _____

2. How many people responded in
   each of the categories?

   _____

   _____

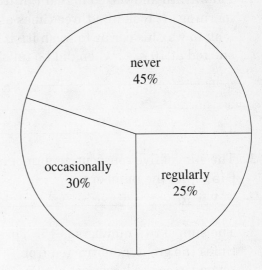

3. What is the sample size?

   _____

4. Can you tell if the sample is random?

   _____

5. Is the question open-option or closed-option?

   _____

Explain why the survey questions in Exercises 6 and 7 are biased.

6. Would you rather buy the TV dinner with a picture of a luscious,
   gourmet meal on it, or one in a plain package?

   _____

   _____

7. Do you want your kids to receive a faulty education by having
   their school day shortened?

   _____

8. A researcher wants to find out what brand of tomato sauce is
   most popular with people who work full-time. He samples
   shoppers at a supermarket between 10 A.M. and 2 P.M. Is this
   a good sample? Explain.

   _____

   _____

9. You decide to run for student council. What factors are important
   to consider if you decide to survey your fellow students?

   _____

   _____

   _____

■■■Practice 1-10 Problem-Solving Strategy:
Too Much or Too Little Information

Use any strategy to solve each problem if possible. Show all your work. If it is not possible to solve the problem, tell why.

1. Pio washed and waxed his car Saturday morning. It took him three times as long to wax his car as to wash it. If he started at 10 A.M., when did he finish?

   _____

   _____

2. Roberto baked twice as many loaves of bread as Mecha did for the bake sale. They both began at noon and finished at 4 P.M. How many loaves did Roberto bake?

   _____

   _____

3. The sum of five consecutive numbers is 645. Find the numbers.

   _____

4. The length of a rectangle is 15 more than the width. The perimeter is 138. Find the length and width. _____

5. The sum of two numbers is 15. Three times the greater subtracted from seven times the lesser equals 15. What are the numbers?

   _____

6. Tom and Florence sold candles for their school. Florence sold more than Tom. If they sold a total of 43 candles, how many candles did Tom sell?

   _____

   _____

7. Fionna bought 3 sweaters on sale for $18.99 each. The sweaters normally sell for $25.95 each. She also bought 2 skirts for $24.99 each. How much did she save by buying the sweaters on sale? _____

8. A photographer is arranging an eighth-grade class for a class photo. He put 10 people in the first row. He then put 6 more people in each row than in the row in front of it. How many students are in eighth grade if he had 9 rows in all? _____

9. Ms. Rhodes had her kindergarten class sorting a pile of buttons. When they separated the pile into groups of 5, there were 3 left over. When they separated the pile into groups of 7, there were 3 left over. When they separated the pile into groups of 9, there were none left over. What is the least number of buttons the students could have had? _____

10. Mark is planning a dinner menu for a party. He can choose from five salads, four main courses, and six desserts. How many different meals does Mark have to choose from?

    _____

Practice 1-11 Probability

A dart is thrown at the game board shown. Find each probability.

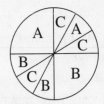

1. $P(A)$ _____   **2.** $P(B)$ _____   **3.** $P(C)$ _____

4. $P(A \text{ or } B)$ _____   **5.** $P(B \text{ or } C)$ _____   **6.** $P(A, B, \text{ or } C)$ _____

A bag of uninflated balloons contains 10 red, 12 blue, 15 yellow, and 8 green balloons. A balloon is drawn at random. Find each probability.

7. $P(\text{red})$ _____   **8.** $P(\text{blue})$ _____   **9.** $P(\text{yellow})$ _____   **10.** $P(\text{green})$ _____

11. What is the probability of picking a balloon that is not yellow? _____

12. What is the probability of picking a balloon that is not red? _____

13. a. You are given a ticket for the weekly drawing at the grocery store each time you enter the store. Last week you were in the store once. There are 1,200 tickets in the box. Find the probability of your winning.

_____

b. Find the probability of your winning if you were in the store three times last week and there are 1,200 tickets in the box.

_____

14. A cheese tray contains slices of Swiss cheese and cheddar cheese. If you randomly pick a slice of cheese, $P(\text{Swiss}) = 0.45$. Find $P(\text{cheddar})$. If there are 200 slices of cheese, how many slices of Swiss cheese are on the tray? _____

15. a. Make a table to find the sample space for tossing two coins.

b. Find the probability that you get one head and one tail when tossing two coins.

_____

▬▬▬*Practice 2-1* Integers and Absolute Value

Write an integer to represent each situation.

1. The top of the world's lowest known active volcano is 160 ft below sea level.

   _____

2. The football team gained three yards on a play.

   _____

3. Jenni owes her friend $20.

   _____

4. The temperature yesterday was five above zero. _____

Use the information in the graph at the right to answer the following.

5. The highest outdoor temperature ever recorded in Nevada, 122°F, was recorded on June 23, 1954. Was it ever that hot in Idaho? Explain.

   _____

   _____

6. Which state had a recorded temperature of 134°F?

   _____

7. The lowest temperature ever recorded in Maine, –48°F, was recorded on January 17, 1925. Was it ever that cold in Minnesota? Explain.

   _____

   _____

8. Which state on the graph had a temperature of 60°F below zero?

   _____

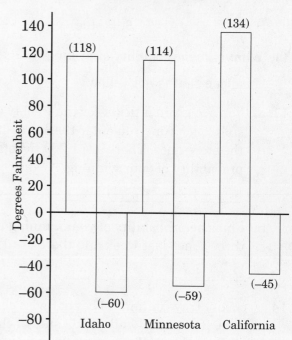

High and Low Temperatures in Selected States

Compare. Write >, <, or =.

9. –12 ☐ 10   10. 9 ☐ –12   11. |4| ☐ |–9| 12. |26| ☐ |–26|

13. |42| ☐ |–93| 14. 53 ☐ –21   15. |6| ☐ 0   16. |9| ☐ |–13|

Order the integers in each set from least to greatest.

17. 0, –5, 5, –15, 15, 25, –25

18. 6, –4, –8, 3, 1, –2, 7

19. 27, –10, –6, –18, 3, 9, –8

20. –3, –7, 7, 4, –9, –4, –1

▰▰▰ *Practice 2-2* Writing and Evaluating
Variable Expressions

Write a variable expression for each word phrase.

1. 5 less than a number

_____

2. 15 more than the absolute value of a
number _____

3. the product of a number and −8

_____

4. 5 more than a number, divided by −9

_____

5. 3 more than the product of 8 and a
number _____

6. 3 less than the absolute value of a
number, times 4 _____

**Write a variable expression for each situation. Explain what
the variable represents.**

7. the amount of money Waldo has if he has $10 more than Jon

_____

8. the amount of money that Mika has if she has some quarters

_____

9. how much weight Kirk can lift if he lifts 30 lb more than his brother

_____

10. how fast Rya runs if she runs 5 mi/h slower than Danae

_____

**Write a word phrase that can be represented by each variable
expression.**

11. $n \div (-4)$

_____

12. $n + 4$

_____

13. $3n$

_____

14. $n - 8$

_____

**Use a calculator, paper and pencil, or mental math to evaluate
each expression for $n = 2$, $x = 6$, and $y = 4$.**

15. $11x + 7$

_____

16. $29y - 15$

_____

17. $6(n + 8)$

_____

18. $(24 \div x) + 18$

_____

19. $(x + n) \div y$

_____

20. $xn + y$

_____

21. $(6 \cdot 8 + y) \cdot n$

_____

22. $6(8 + y) \cdot n$

_____

23. $6 \cdot 8 + y \cdot n$

_____

24. $y + n \cdot n$

_____

25. $12 \div x + xy$

_____

26. $(2n + 2y) \div 2x$

_____

Practice 2-3 Adding Integers

Write the addition equation that is suggested by each model.

1.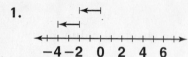

   _____

2.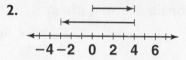

   _____

3.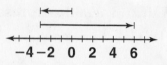

   _____

4.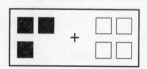

   _____

5.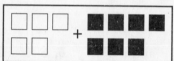

   _____

6.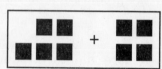

   _____

Write an equation to find the sum for each situation.

7. The varsity football team gained 7 yd on one play and then lost 4 yd.

   _____

8. The airplane descended 140 ft and then rose 112 ft.

   _____

9. The squirrel climbed 18 in. up a tree, slipped back 4 in., and then climbed up 12 in. more.

   _____

10. The temperature was 72°F at noon. At midnight a cold front moved in, dropping the temperature 12°F.

    _____

Find each sum.

11. $8 + (7)$

12. $9 + (-4)$

13. $-6 + (-8)$

14. $8 + (-14)$

15. $9 + (-17)$

16. $-15 + (-11)$

17. $-23 + 18$

18. $-19 + 16$

19. $27 + 34$

20. $-8 + (-17)$

21. $19 + (-8)$

22. $23 + (-31)$

23. $-16 + (-16)$

24. $24 + (-16)$

25. $-14 + (-19)$

26. $-30 + 20$

27. $40 + 20$

28. $-18 + (-20)$

29. $42 + (-17)$

30. $-17 + (-16)$

31. Jill and Joe are playing a game. The chart at the right shows the points gained or lost on each round.

    a. Who has the most points after the fifth round?

    _____

    b. To win, a player must have 20 points. How many points does each player need to win?

    _____

Round	Jill	Joe
1	10	12
2	-2	3
3	6	-8
4	4	0
5	-2	7

Practice 2-4 Subtracting Integers

Draw an algebra tile model to find each difference.

1. $6 - (-2)$ _____   **2.** $7 - 8$ _____   **3.** $-4 - (-3)$ _____

Without performing the subtraction, state whether the difference will be positive or negative.

4. $-8 - (-6)$ _____   **5.** $23 - 42$ _____   **6.** $6 - (-8)$ _____   **7.** $-16 - (-24)$ _____

Write an equivalent addition expression for each subtraction expression. Then find the difference.

8. $17 - 12$ _____   **9.** $19 - 21$ _____   **10.** $-14 - 10$ _____   **11.** $53 - (-10)$ _____

12. $-9 - 14$ _____   **13.** $23 - 36$ _____   **14.** $-2 - (-8)$ _____   **15.** $28 - (-4)$ _____

16. $-23 - 14$ _____   **17.** $-23 - (-14)$ _____   **18.** $0 - (-11)$ _____   **19.** $43 - 28$ _____

20. $28 - 43$ _____   **21.** $26 - 17$ _____   **22.** $-26 - 17$ _____   **23.** $33 - (-14)$ _____

24. $-14 - 33$ _____   **25.** $-32 - (-18)$ _____   **26.** $-15 - (-26)$ _____   **27.** $32 - (-16)$ _____

28. $-19 - (-12)$ _____   **29.** $-16 - (-21)$ _____   **30.** $27 - 19$ _____   **31.** $-14 - 27$ _____

Evaluate each expression for $x = 5$, $y = -6$, and $z = -7$.

32. $x + y$ _____   **33.** $15 - z$ _____   **34.** $y - z$ _____   **35.** $x + y - z$ _____

36. $y - 15 + x$ _____   **37.** $32 - z + x$ _____   **38.** $|x| - |y|$ _____   **39.** $z + |x|$ _____

Write the next four numbers in each pattern.

40. 52, 46, 40, _____   **41.** 7, 4, 1, _____

42. 12, 6, 0, _____   **43.** 8, 5, 6, 3, 4, 1, _____

■■■■ Practice 2-5 *Multiplying and Dividing Integers*

Write two related division equations for each multiplication equation.

1. $4 \cdot (-3) = -12$ **2.** $-9 \cdot (-8) = 72$ **3.** $7 \cdot (-6) = -42$

_____   _____   _____

_____   _____   _____

4. $-3 \cdot 5 = -15$ **5.** $9 \cdot (-4) = -36$ **6.** $-6 \cdot 8 = -48$

_____   _____   _____

_____   _____   _____

Find each product or quotient.

7. $-4 \cdot 8$ **8.** $-7 \cdot (-9)$ **9.** $-5 \cdot (-11)$ **10.** $20 \cdot (-3)$

_____   _____   _____   _____

11. $2(-3)(-3)$ **12.** $(-4)(-4)(-4)$ **13.** $(-3)(4)(-5)$ **14.** $(5)(2)(-20)$

_____   _____   _____   _____

15. $-63 \div 7$ **16.** $81 \div (-9)$ **17.** $-77 \div 7$ **18.** $96 \div (-12)$

_____   _____   _____   _____

19. $-54 \div (-6)$ **20.** $-120 \div 10$ **21.** $-1000 \div (-100)$ **22.** $540 \div (-90)$

_____   _____   _____   _____

You want to find a route from Start to Finish. Evaluate the expression in each square. You can only move to the right or down, and you can only move to a square that has an answer greater than the expression in your current square. Draw a line through the route you will take.

Start

$-9(26)$	$-29 - 146$	$-25 + (-100)$	$-9(40)$	$8(7)$	$23 + (-9)$
$-10(27)$	$-800 - 92$	$200 \div (-2)$	$-40 + 12$	$-600 \div 6$	$21(16)$
$-26 - 19$	$-90 - 15$	$400 \div (-2)$	$17 - 19$	$-4\,(8)$	$200 \div 4$
$-17 -(-24)$	$17(11)$	$500 \div (-4)$	$5(0)$	$8 - (-27)$	$47 + 1$

Finish

Practice 2-6 Exponents and Multiplication

Write each expression using exponents.

1. $8 \cdot 8 \cdot 8 \cdot 8 \cdot 8$ _____

2. $(-2)(-2)(-2)(-2)$ _____

3. $x \cdot x \cdot x \cdot x \cdot x \cdot x$ _____

4. $(-3m)(-3m)(-3m)$ _____

5. $4 \cdot t \cdot t \cdot t$ _____

6. $(5v)(5v)(5v)(5v)(5v)$ _____

Write each expression as a product of the same factor.

7. a^2 _____

8. 19^3 _____

9. -6^2 _____

10. $-x^3$ _____

Evaluate each power.

11. $(-5)^4$ _____

12. 4^3 _____

13. -10^2 _____

14. 20^1 _____

Write each expression using a single exponent.

15. $3^2 \cdot 3^5$ _____

16. $1^3 \cdot 1^4$ _____

17. $5^4 \cdot 5^3$ _____

18. $(-3)^2 \cdot (-3)^3$ _____

19. $a^1 \cdot a^2$ _____

20. $(-y)^3 \cdot (-y)^2$ _____

21. $-z^3 \cdot z^9$ _____

22. $x^2 \cdot x^7$ _____

Evaluate each expression for the given value.

23. $4x^2$ for $x = 3$ _____

24. $(5b)^2$ for $b = 2$ _____

25. $-6x^2$ for $x = 3$ _____

26. $(-3g)^2$ for $g = 2$ _____

Choose a calculator, paper and pencil, or mental math to evaluate each expression.

27. 3^5 _____

28. -2^4 _____

29. -10^3 _____

30. -8^3 _____

Choose A, B, C, or D.

31. In Westville, there is a house. In the house, there are 6 people. Each person in the house has 6 pets. Which of the following expressions represents the total number of people and pets? Explain your answer.

   A. 6^3 **B.** $3(6)$ **C.** 63 **D.** $6^2 + 6$

   _____

   _____

▬▬▬**Practice 2-7** *Evaluating Expressions with Exponents*

Evaluate each expression.

1. $(-4)^2 + 10 \cdot 2$ **2.** $-4^2 + 10 \cdot 2$ **3.** $(5 \cdot 3)^2 + 8$

_____   _____   _____

4. $5 \cdot 3^2 + 8$ **5.** $9 + (7 - 4)^2$ **6.** $-9 + 7 - 4^2$

_____   _____   _____

7. $(-6)^2 + 3^3 - 7$ **8.** $-6^2 + 3^3 - 7$ **9.** $2^3 + (8 - 5) \cdot 4 - 5^2$

_____   _____   _____

10. $(2^3 + 8) - 5 \cdot 4 - 5^2$ **11.** $2^3 \cdot 3 - 5 \cdot 5^2 + 8$ **12.** $2^3 \cdot 3 - 5(5^2 + 8)$

_____   _____   _____

Evaluate each expression for the given value of the variable.

13. $7x^3$; $x = 2$ **14.** $-5m^2$; $m = 4$ **15.** $2y^2 + 3y + 8$; $y = -5$

_____   _____   _____

16. $3 \cdot b^3$; $b = 3$ **17.** $-6n^3 \div 8$; $n = -2$ **18.** $-3x^2y$; $x = 2, y = 5$

_____   _____   _____

Choose a calculator, paper and pencil, or mental math. Evaluate each expression for $x = -3.5$, $y = -2$, and $z = 3$.

19. $y^2 + 8$ **20.** $x^3 - 2$ **21.** $8 - z^3$ **22.** $10x^2y^2$

_____   _____   _____   _____

23. $x^3y^3z^3$ **24.** $z \div (-z)$ **25.** $y^2 \div (-y)$ **26.** $(x - z)^2$

_____   _____   _____   _____

Estimate each expression for the given value, then find the exact value using a calculator or pencil and paper.

27. $7 + 3q$; $q = 7.6$ **28.** $j^2 + 6$; $j = 4.7$ **29.** $2m^2 - 3m$; $m = 1.6$

_____   _____   _____

30. $y^2 - 19y + 16$; $y = 2.5$ **31.** $x^2 + 7x - 19$; $x = 4.21$ **32.** $v^2 + v$; $v = 9.8$

_____   _____   _____

Solve.

33. Suppose you own a card shop. You buy one line of cards at a rate of 4 cards for $5. You plan to sell the cards at a rate of 3 cards for $5. How many cards must you sell in order to make a profit of $100? _____

◼◼ *Practice 2-8* Mental Math and Properties of Numbers

Evaluate each sum mentally.

1. $8 + (-2) + 7 + (-5)$

2. $-7 + 9 + 11 + (-13)$

3. $17 + (-9) + 18 + (-11)$

_____

4. $65 + 23 + 35$

5. $220 + 343 + 80$

6. $230 + 170 + 18 + (-5)$

_____

Evaluate each product mentally.

7. $(-5)(38)(-20)$

8. $2 \cdot 83 \cdot (-5)$

9. $-5 \cdot (2 \cdot 38)$

_____

10. $4 \cdot (25 \cdot 27)$

11. $(50)(86)(20)$

12. $-4 \cdot (36 \cdot 5)$

_____

Rewrite each product so you can use the distributive property. Evaluate mentally.

13. $25(-99)$

14. $19(-6)$

15. $6 \cdot \$2.99$

_____

16. $102 \cdot \$21$

17. $19 \cdot 21$

18. $26 \cdot 97$

_____

19. $21 \cdot (-11)$

20. $9 \cdot \$4.98$

21. $103 \cdot \$32$

_____

Decide whether the statement is true or false.

22. $9 \cdot 8 + 6 = 9 \cdot 6 + 8$

23. $-7(11 - 4) = 7(15)$

_____

24. $12 \cdot 7 = 10 \cdot 7 + 2 \cdot 7$

25. $15 + (-17) = -17 + 15$

_____

26. $93 \cdot (-8) = -93 \cdot 8$

27. $53 + (-19) = -53 + 19$

_____

28. Complete the triangle of numbers by looking for a pattern.

```
                        2
                   2         2
               2        4        2
           2       ___       8       2
       2       16       64      ___      2
   2      ___      ___      ___      32      2
```

▬▬▬ *Practice 2-9* Problem-Solving Strategy: Guess and Test

Use *Guess and Test* to solve each problem.

1. Philip drove 1,096 miles in two days. He drove 240 miles more on the second day than he drove on the first day. How many miles did he drive each day? _____

2. Bea raised some cows and some turkeys. She raised a total of 28 cows and turkeys. There were 96 legs in all. How many cows and how many turkeys did Bea raise? _____

3. Two integers have a difference of –11 and a sum of –3. What are the integers? _____

4. Tickets for a benefit dinner were on sale for three weeks. Twice as many tickets were sold during the third week as were sold during the first two weeks combined. If a total of 1,095 tickets were sold, how many were sold the third week? _____

Choose any strategy to solve each problem. Show all your work.

5. A stuffed bear is sold with either 1 or 2 cubs. A batch of 20 cubs is to be sent to a local store. How many different combinations of either 1 or 2 cubs could there be?

   _____

6. Priya ordered twice as many blankets as she did quilts for the department store where she works. The order was for 126 items. How many blankets and how many quilts did Priya order?

   _____

7. Kent is three years older than his sister Debbie. The sum of their ages is 105. Find their ages.

   _____

8. A bowling league has 16 teams. During a single-elimination tournament, the winner of each match goes on to the next round. How many matches does the winning team need to play?

   _____

9. In the addition problems below, each letter represents the same digit in both problems. Replace each letter with a different digit, 1 through 9, so that both addition problems are true. (There are two possible answers.)

   $$\begin{array}{r} A\,B\,C \\ +\,D\,E\,F \\ \hline G\,H\,I \end{array} \qquad \begin{array}{r} A\,D\,G \\ +\,B\,E\,H \\ \hline C\,F\,I \end{array}$$

Practice 2-10 Exponents and Division

Write each expression as an integer or simple fraction.

1. 8^{-2} _____   **2.** $(-3)^0$ _____   **3.** 5^{-1} _____   **4.** 18^0 _____

5. 2^{-5} _____   **6.** 3^{-3} _____   **7.** 2^{-3} _____   **8.** 5^{-2} _____

Choose a calculator, paper and pencil, or mental math to simplify each expression. Give the answer as an integer or simple fraction.

9. $\frac{4^4}{4}$ _____   **10.** $8^6 \div 8^8$ _____   **11.** $\frac{(-3)^6}{(-3)^8}$ _____   **12.** $\frac{8^4}{8^0}$ _____

13. $1^{15} \div 1^{18}$ _____   **14.** $7 \div 7^4$ _____   **15.** $\frac{(-4)^8}{(-4)^4}$ _____   **16.** $\frac{10^9}{10^{12}}$ _____

17. $\frac{7^5}{7^3}$ _____   **18.** $8^4 \div 8^2$ _____   **19.** $\frac{(-3)^5}{(-3)^8}$ _____   **20.** $\frac{6^7}{6^8}$ _____

Simplify each quotient, using a positive exponent. Assume each variable does not equal zero.

21. $\frac{b^{12}}{b^4}$ _____   **22.** $\frac{g^9}{g^{15}}$ _____   **23.** $x^{16} \div x^7$ _____   **24.** $v^{20} \div v^{25}$ _____

Complete each equation.

25. $\frac{1}{3^5} = 3^{\blacksquare}$ **26.** $\frac{1}{(-2)^7} = -2^{\blacksquare}$ **27.** $\frac{1}{x^2} = x^{\blacksquare}$ **28.** $\frac{1}{-125} = (-5)^{\blacksquare}$

_____   _____   _____   _____

29. $\frac{1}{1,000} = 10^{\blacksquare}$ **30.** $\frac{5^{10}}{\blacksquare} = 5^5$ **31.** $\frac{z^{\blacksquare}}{z^8} = z^{-3}$ **32.** $\frac{q^5}{\blacksquare} = q^{-7}$

_____   _____   _____   _____

Write each number as a power of 10.

33. 100,000   **34.** 0.00000001   **35.** 100,000,000

_____   _____   _____

36. 100,000,000,000   **37.** 0.0000000001   **38.** 1.0

_____   _____   _____

39. Write each term as a power of 4, and write the next three terms of the sequence 256, 64, 16, 4, ...

_____

◼◼◼Practice 2-11 *Scientific Notation*

Write each number in scientific notation.

1. 45   **2.** 250   **3.** 0.9   **4.** 0.02

5. 670   **6.** 0.041   **7.** 500   **8.** 0.0003

9. 43,200   **10.** 0.0971   **11.** 38,050   **12.** 0.902

13. 480,000   **14.** 0.000096   **15.** 8,750,000   **16.** 0.0000407

Write each number in standard form.

17. 3.1×10^1 **18.** 8.07×10^{-2} **19.** 4.96×10^3 **20.** 8.073×10^{-2}

21. 4.501×10^4 **22.** 9.7×10^{-6} **23.** 8.3×10^{-7} **24.** 3.42×10^4

25. 2.86×10^5 **26.** 3.58×10^{-6} **27.** 8.1×10^{-1} **28.** 9.071×10^{-2}

29. 4.83×10^9 **30.** 2.73×10^8 **31.** 2.57×10^{-5} **32.** 8.09×10^{-4}

Circle A, B, C, or D. Which set is ordered from least to greatest?

33. **A.** 8.9×10^{-2}, 6.3×10^3, 2.1×10^4, 7.8×10^{-5}

    B. 2.1×10^4, 6.3×10^3, 7.8×10^{-5}, 8.9×10^{-2}

    C. 7.8×10^{-5}, 8.9×10^{-2}, 6.3×10^3, 2.1×10^4

    D. 8.9×10^{-2}, 7.8×10^{-5}, 6.3×10^3, 2.1×10^4

Write each number using scientific notation.

34. The eye's retina contains about 130 million light-sensitive cells.

35. A mulberry silkworm can spin a single thread that measures up to 3,900 ft in length. _____

36. The ear holds the smallest muscle, measuring 0.04 in. long.

37. Hair can grow approximately 0.013 in. per day.

Practice 3-1 *Simplifying Variable Expressions*

Simplify each expression.

1. $4a + 7 + 2a$

2. $8(k - 9)$

3. $5n + 6n - 2n$

4. $(w + 3)7$

5. $5(b - 6) + 9$

6. $-4 + 8(2 + t)$

7. $-4 + 3(6 + k)$

8. $12j - 9j$

9. $6(d - 8)$

10. $-9 + 8(x + 6)$

11. $4(m + 6) - 3$

12. $27 + 2(f - 19)$

13. $4v - 7 + 8v + 4 - 5$

14. $5(g + 8) + 7 + 4g$

15. $12h - 17 - h + 16 - 2h$

16. $7(e - 8) + 12 - 2e$

17. $-3y + 7 + y + 6y$

18. $(3.2m + 1.8) - 1.07m$

Choose a calculator, paper and pencil, or mental math to simplify each expression.

19. $28k + 36(7 + k)$

20. $3.09(j + 4.6)$

21. $12b + 24(b - 42)$

22. $7.9y + 8.4 - 2.04y$

23. $4.3(5.6 + c)$

24. $83x + 15(x - 17)$

25. $9.8c + 8d - 4.6c + 2.9d$

26. $18 + 27m - 29 + 36m$

27. $8(j + 12) + 4(k - 19)$

28. $4.2r + 8.1s + 1.09r + 6.32s$

29. $43 + 16c - 18d + 56c + 16d$

30. $9(a + 14) + 8(b - 16)$

31. Tyrone bought 15.3 gal of gasoline priced at g dollars per gal, 2 qt of oil priced at q dollars per qt, and a wiper blade priced at $3.79. Write an expression that represents the total cost of these items.

32. Choose a number. Multiply by 2. Add 6 to the product. Divide by 2. Then subtract 3. What is the answer? Repeat this process using two different numbers. Explain what happened.

Practice 3-2 Solving Equations by Subtracting or Adding

Choose a calculator, paper and pencil, or mental math to solve each equation. Check the solution.

1. $x - 6 = -18$

2. $-14 = 8 + j$

3. $4.19 + w = 19.72$

4. $b + \frac{1}{6} = \frac{7}{8}$

5. $9 + k = 27$

6. $14 + t = -17$

7. $v - 2.59 = 26$

8. $r + 9 = 15$

9. $n - 19 = 26$

10. $14 = -3 + s$

11. $9 = d - 4.3$

12. $g - \frac{1}{4} = \frac{5}{8}$

13. $15 + y = -4$

14. $8.17 + d = 14.2$

15. $f - 19 = 14$

16. $-19 = a - 14$

17. $-2 = g + 21$

18. $h - 9.2 = 7.3$

19. $c - 9.02 = -8.6$

20. $b + 31 = -8$

21. $14 = i - 27$

22. $-41 = n - 18$

23. $p + \frac{3}{4} = \frac{9}{10}$

24. $-4 = w + 16$

Write an equation for each problem. Solve the equation. Then give the solution of the problem.

25. Yesterday Josh sold some boxes of greeting cards. Today he sold seven boxes. If he sold 25 boxes in all, how many did he sell yesterday?

26. After Hoshi spent $27.98 for a sweater, she had $18.76 left. How much money did she have to begin with?

27. After Simon donated four books to the school library, he had 28 books left. How many books did Simon have to start with?

28. One day Reeva baked several dozen muffins. The next day she made 8 dozen more muffins. If she made 20 dozen muffins in all, how many dozen did she make the first day?

Practice 3-3 Solving Equations by Dividing or Multiplying

Choose a calculator, paper and pencil, or mental math to solve each equation. Check the solution.

1. $\dfrac{a}{-6} = 2$

2. $18 = \dfrac{v}{-1.8}$

3. $46 = 2.3m$

4. $-114 = -6k$

5. $0 = \dfrac{b}{19}$

6. $136 = 8y$

7. $0.6j = -1.44$

8. $\dfrac{q}{7.4} = 8.3$

9. $28b = -131.6$

10. $\dfrac{n}{-9} = -107$

11. $37c = -777$

12. $\dfrac{n}{-1.28} = 4.96$

13. $53k = -3,816$

14. $\dfrac{e}{-8.6} = -9.04$

15. $-12j = 90$

16. $\dfrac{q}{7.4} = -8.9$

17. $5.7b = 11.742$

18. $\dfrac{c}{-19} = 25$

19. $43b = -3,397$

20. $\dfrac{s}{-19.6} = 2.04$

21. $-8.05d = 198.03$

22. $\dfrac{f}{87} = 93$

23. $56.4w = 163.56$

24. $\dfrac{g}{-47} = 105$

25. $\dfrac{b}{-7} = 17$

26. $12z = -60$

27. $\dfrac{k}{9.2} = 7.6$

28. $17y = -153$

Write an equation for each problem. Solve the equation. Then give the solution of the problem.

29. Twelve notebooks cost $15.48 in all. What is the price of one notebook?

30. Skylar bought seven books at $12.95 each. How much did Skylar spend?

31. Clarinda has to make 96 treats for school. How many dozen treats is this?

32. Eugenio has five payments left to make on his computer. If each payment is $157.90, how much does he still owe?

Course 3 Chapter 3

Practice 3-4 Solving Two-Step Equations

Choose a calculator, paper and pencil, or mental math to solve each equation. Check the solution.

1. $4r + 6 = 14$

2. $9y - 11 = 7$

3. $\frac{m}{4} + 6 = 3$

4. $\frac{k}{-9} + 6 = -4$

5. $-5b - 6 = -11$

6. $\frac{v}{-7} + 8 = 19$

7. $3.4t + 19.36 = -10.22$

8. $\frac{n}{-1.6} + 7.9 = 8.4$

9. $4.6b + 26.8 = 50.72$

10. $\frac{a}{-8.06} + 7.02 = 18.4$

11. $-2.06d + 18 = -10.84$

12. $\frac{e}{-95} + 6 = 4$

13. $-9i - 17 = -26$

14. $\frac{j}{-1.9} + 2.7 = -8.6$

15. $14.9 = 8.6 + 0.9m$

16. $84 = 19 + \frac{z}{12}$

17. $15w - 21 = -111$

18. $-12.4 = -19.1 + \frac{n}{-7.9}$

19. Hugo received $100 for his birthday. He then saved $20 per week until he had a total of $460 to buy a printer. Use an equation to show how many weeks it took him to save the money.

20. A health club charges a $50 initial fee plus $2 for each visit. Moselle has spent a total of $144 at the health club this year. Use an equation to find how many visits she has made.

Solve each equation to find the value of the variable. Write the answer in the puzzle. Do not include any negative signs or any decimal points.

Across

1. $6n - 12 = 2.4$

2. $\frac{n}{3} + 4.6 = 21.6$

4. $x - 3 = 51.29$

6. $2z + 2 = 7.6$

Down

1. $\frac{j}{5} - 14 = -9$

2. $3x - 2 = 169$

3. $\frac{x}{4} + 1 = 19$

4. $\frac{x}{3} + 4 = 22$

5. $2x - 2 = 182$

Practice 3-5 Problem-Solving Strategy: Write an Equation

Write an equation to solve each problem. Check the solution.

1. The cost of a long-distance phone call is $.56 for the first minute and $.32 for each additional minute. What was the total length of a call that cost $9.20?

_____

2. A house sits on a rectangular piece of land. Two of the sides measure 104 ft each. If all four sides add to 576 ft, how long is each of the other two sides?

_____

3. A gas tank contains 12.6 gal of gas. If this is $\frac{4}{5}$ of the gas tank's capacity, how many gallons can the tank hold?

_____

4. If you subtract 9.4 from a third of a number, the result is 8.7. What is the number?

_____

Choose any strategy to solve each problem. Show all your work.

5. Mary and Jim have tickets to a concert. Mary's ticket number is one less than Jim's ticket number. The product of their numbers is 812. What are the two numbers?

_____

6. The Beards' budget is shown at the right. Their house payment is raised $120. Their income will be no more than it is now, so they plan on subtracting an equal amount from each of the other categories. How much will be available to spend on bills?

Beards' Budget	
Item	Amount
House	$650
Food	$300
Bills	$250
Other	$140

_____

7. Antonio watches $\frac{2}{3}$ of a movie at home and then decides to finish watching it later. If he already has watched 2 hours of the movie, how long is it?

_____

Practice 3-6 Simplifying and Solving Equations

Write an equation that can be modeled by the tiles. Solve the equation.

1.

_____

2.

_____

Choose a calculator, paper and pencil, or mental math to solve each equation. Check the solution.

3. $2(2.5b - 9) + 6b = -7$

_____

4. $12y = 2y + 40$

_____

5. $6(c + 4) = 4c - 18$

_____

6. $0.7w + 16 + 4w = 27.28$

_____

7. $24 = -6(m + 1) + 18$

_____

8. $0.5m + 6.4 = 4.9 - 0.1m$

_____

9. $7k - 8 + 2(k + 12) = 52$

_____

10. $14b = 16(b + 12)$

_____

11. $4(1.5c + 6) - 2c = -9$

_____

12. $7y = y - 42$

_____

13. $9(d - 4) = 5d + 8$

_____

14. $0.5n + 17 + n = 20$

_____

15. $20 = -4(f + 6) + 14$

_____

16. $12j = 16(j - 8)$

_____

17. $0.7p + 4.6 = 7.3 - 0.2p$

_____

18. $9a - 4 + 3(a - 11) = 23$

_____

19. $6(f + 5) = 2f - 8$

_____

20. $15p = 6(p - 9)$

_____

21. $0.5t + 4.1 = 5.7 - 0.3t$

_____

22. $9q - 14 + 3(q - 8) = 7$

_____

Practice 3-7 Formulas

Write appropriate formulas to find the perimeter and area of each figure. Then find the perimeter and area of each figure.

1.

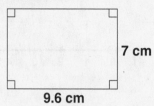

7 cm

9.6 cm

_____

_____

2.

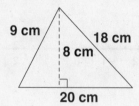

9 cm   18 cm

8 cm

20 cm

_____

_____

3.

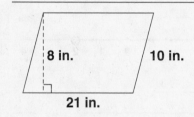

8 in.   10 in.

21 in.

_____

_____

4.

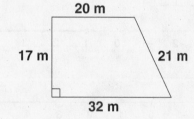

20 m

17 m   21 m

32 m

_____

_____

Write an equation to find the the solution for each problem. Solve the equation. Then give the solution for the problem.

5. The Kents left home at 7:00 A.M. and drove to their parents' house 400 mi away. They arrived at 3:00 P.M. What was their average speed?

_____

6. An airplane flew for 4 h 30 min at an average speed of 515 mi/h. How far did it fly?

_____

7. Marcia rowed her boat 18 mi downstream at a rate of 12 mi/h. How long did the trip take?

_____

In Exercises 8–11, use the formula $F = \frac{9}{5}C + 32$ or $C = \frac{5}{9}(F - 32)$ to find a temperature in either degrees Fahrenheit, °F, or degrees Celsius, °C.

8. What is the temperature in degrees Fahrenheit when it is 0° C?

_____

9. What is the temperature in degrees Fahrenheit when it is 100° C?

_____

10. What is the temperature in degrees Celsius when it is −4° F?

_____

11. What is the temperature in degrees Celsius when it is 77° F?

_____

Course 3 Chapter 3

Practice 3-8 Inequalities

Write an inequality for each graph.

1.
```
  -4 -3 -2 -1  0  1  2  3  4
```
_____

2.
```
  -2 -1  0  1  2  3  4  5  6
```
_____

3.
```
  -4 -3 -2 -1  0  1  2
```
_____

4.
```
  -3 -2 -1  0  1  2  3  4
```
_____

5.
```
  -3 -2 -1  0  1  2  3
```
_____

6.
```
  -4 -3 -2 -1  0  1
```
_____

7.
```
  -3 -2 -1  0  1  2  3
```
_____

8.
```
  -3 -2 -1  0  1  2  3  4
```
_____

9.
```
  -2 -1  0  1  2  3  4
```
_____

10.
```
  -3 -2 -1  0  1  2  3
```
_____

Graph each inequality on a number line.

11. $x \geq -6$

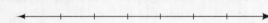

12. $x < 5$

13. $x < -5$

14. $x \geq -1$

15. $x \leq 0$

16. $x > -2$

17. $x \leq 7$

18. $x \geq -5$

Name _____ Class _____ Date _____

Solving Inequalities by Subtracting
or Adding

Solve each inequality. Graph the solution.

1. $m + 6 > 2$

_____

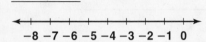

2. $q + 4 \leq 9$

_____

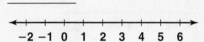

3. $w - 6 > -9$

_____

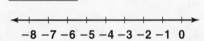

4. $y - 3 < -4$

_____

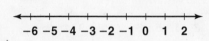

5. $k + 9 \leq 12$

_____

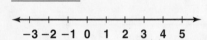

6. $u + 6 \geq 8$

_____

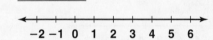

7. $x - 9 < -12$

_____

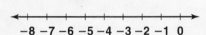

8. $d + 9 \geq 10$

_____

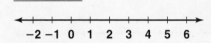

9. $h - 12 < -15$

_____

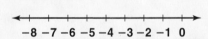

10. $e + 14 \geq 24$

_____

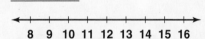

11. $g - 9.6 \leq -4.6$

_____

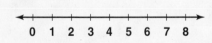

12. $r + 7.1 > 2.1$

_____

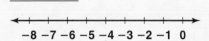

**Write an inequality for each problem. Solve the
inequality. Then give the solution of the problem.**

13. The amount of snow on the ground
increased by 8 in. between 7 P.M. and
10 P.M. By 10 P.M., there was less than
2 ft of snow. How much snow was
there by 7 P.M.?

_____

14. The school record for points scored in
a basketball season by one player is
462. Maria has 235 points so far this
season. How many more points does
she need to break the record?

_____

Course 3 Chapter 3

■■■■ Practice 3-10 *Solving Inequalities by Dividing or Multiplying*

Solve each inequality. Graph the solution.

1. $-5m < 20$

_____

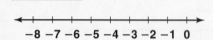

2. $\frac{j}{6} \leq 0$

_____

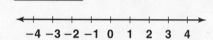

3. $4v > 16$

_____

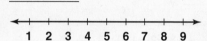

4. $\frac{b}{2} < 4$

_____

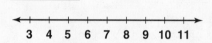

5. $5a > -10$

_____

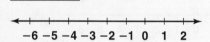

6. $\frac{c}{-3} \geq 6$

_____

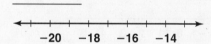

7. $\frac{c}{-6} > 1$

_____

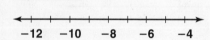

8. $-4i \leq -16$

_____

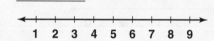

9. $5d < -75$

_____

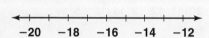

10. $\frac{d}{12} < -1$

_____

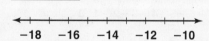

11. $0.5n \geq -2.5$

_____

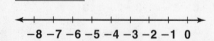

12. $\frac{p}{0.2} \leq 10$

_____

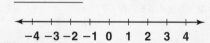

Write an inequality for each problem. Solve the inequality. Then give the solution of the problem.

13. Dom wants to buy 5 baseballs. He has $20. What is the most each baseball can cost?

_____

14. A typing service charges $5.00 per page. Mrs. Garza does not want to spend more than $50 for the typing. What is the maximum number of pages she can have typed?

_____

Name _____ Class _____ Date _____

Practice 4-1 Graphing Points

Name the point with the given coordinates.

1. $(-4, 3)$ _____

2. $(7, 4)$ _____

3. $(0, -5)$ _____

4. $(5, -3)$ _____

5. $(4, -6)$ _____

6. $(6, 0)$ _____

7. $(4, 3)$ _____

8. $(-3, -4)$ _____

Name the coordinates of each point.

9. J _____

10. R _____

11. K _____

12. M _____

13. I _____

14. P _____

15. N _____

16. L _____

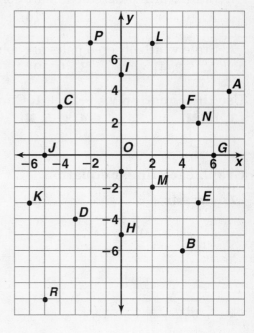

In Exercises 17–28, state in which quadrant or on which axis you would find the point with the given coordinates.

17. $(-3, -2)$

18. $(7, 0)$

19. $(4, 0)$

20. $(-3, -9)$

_____

_____

_____

_____

21. $(4, -7)$

22. $(7, -5)$

23. $(2, 9)$

24. $(0, 9)$

_____

_____

_____

_____

25. $(0, -6)$

26. $(4, 2)$

27. $(-3, 2)$

28. $(0, 0)$

_____

_____

_____

_____

29. Arnie plotted points on the graph at the right. He placed his pencil point at A. He can move either right or down any number of units until he reaches point B. In how many ways can he do this?

_____

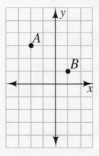

30. Marika had to draw $\triangle ABC$ that fit several requirements.
    a. It must fit in the box shown.
    b. The base $\overline{AB}$ has coordinates $A(-2, 0)$ and $B(2, 0)$.
    c. Point C must be on the y-axis.
    Name all the points that could be point C.

_____

_____

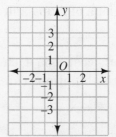

Practice 4-2 Equations with Two Variables

1. State which ordered pairs are solutions of $y = 3x - 8$. _____
   A. $(0, -8)$ **B.** $(6, -10)$ **C.** $(-2, -2)$ **D.** $(4, 4)$

2. State which ordered pairs are solutions of $y = -5x + 19$. _____
   A. $(-3, 4)$ **B.** $(0, 19)$ **C.** $(2, 9)$ **D.** $(-4, 39)$

Use the equation $y = -2x + 1$. Complete each solution.

3. $(0, \blacksquare)$ 4. $(-5, \blacksquare)$ 5. $(20, \blacksquare)$ 6. $(-68, \blacksquare)$

_____   _____   _____   _____

Graph each linear equation.

7. $y = -4x + 6$ 8. $y = \frac{5}{2}x - 5$ 9. $y = -\frac{1}{2}x + 3$

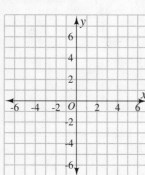 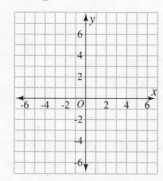 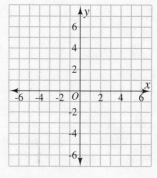

10. $y = \frac{1}{2}x - \frac{1}{2}$ 11. $y = -2x + 7$ 12. $y = -3x - 1$

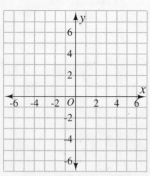 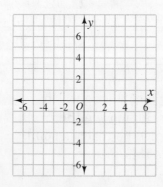 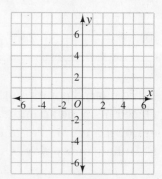

13. Jan wants to buy both maps and atlases for her trip. The maps cost $2.00 each, and the atlases cost $5.00 each. For what combinations of maps and atlases can she spend $25.00?

_____

14. Grapefruits cost $.65 each and oranges cost $.20 each. What possible combinations can Keiko buy for exactly $5.00?

_____

Practice 4-3 Understanding Slope

Find the slope of each line.

1.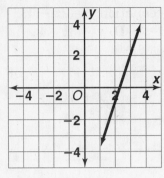

2.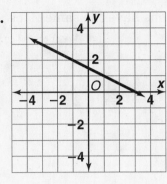

3.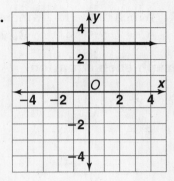

_____

_____

_____

Find the slope of each line. Describe how one variable changes in relation to the other.

4.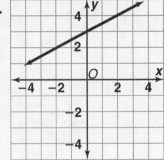

5.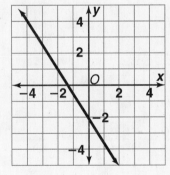

_____

_____

_____

_____

The points from each table lie on a line. Find the slope of the line. Then graph each line on the grid shown.

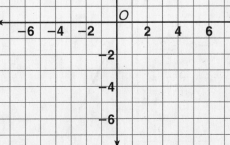

6.

x	0	1	2	3	4
y	−3	−1	1	3	5

slope = _____

7.

x	0	1	2	3	4
y	5	3	1	−1	−3

slope = _____

Practice 4-4 Using the y-intercept

Circle A, B, C, or D.

1. Which of the following equations have the same slope as the equation $y = 2x - 4$?
   A. $y = 2x + 4$ **B.** $y = -2x + 3$ **C.** $y = 4x - 2$ **D.** $y = 3x - 4$

Graph each equation.

2. $y = \frac{3}{4}x - 3$

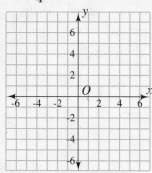

3. $y = -\frac{2}{5}x + 2$

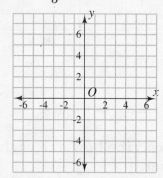

4. $y = -\frac{4}{3}x + 4$

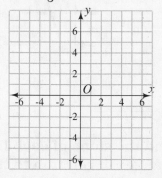

5. $y = \frac{4}{5}x + 4$

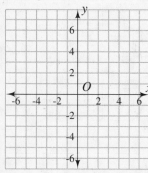

6. $y = x + 4$

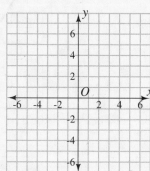

7. $y = \frac{5}{3}x - 5$

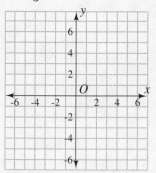

Write an equation for each line. Use slope-intercept form.

8.

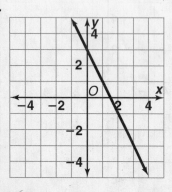

_____

9.

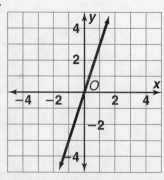

_____

10.

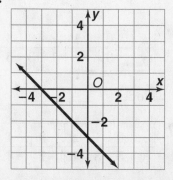

_____

Practice 4-5 Problem-Solving Strategy: Use Logical Reasoning

Use logical reasoning to solve each problem.

Factors
32: 1, 2, 4, 8, 16, 32
24: 1, 2, 3, 4, 6, 8, 12, 24

1. Place the factors of 32 and 24 in a Venn diagram. What are the common factors of 32 and 24? What is the greatest common factor? _____

2. Twenty-six students were asked if they play a sport or are in the band. Eighteen students play a sport and 15 are in the band. Four students do neither. How many students do both?

   _____

3. A favorite-sport poll of 30 teenagers shows that 18 like soccer, 9 like baseball, and 10 like ice hockey. Three teenagers like all three sports, 3 like only soccer and baseball, 4 like only hockey and soccer, and 3 like only hockey. How many teenagers do not like any of these sports? _____

4. A survey on favorite kinds of books shows that 9 people like mysteries, 10 like adventure stories, and 8 enjoy biographies. Three of the people read only mysteries and adventure stories, 4 read only adventure stories and biographies, 4 read only mysteries and 2 read all three kinds of books. How many people were surveyed? _____

Use any strategy to solve each problem.

5. Marcy plans to save $3 in January, $4 in February, $6 in March, and $9 in April. If she continues this pattern, how much money will she save in December? _____

6. Inez is building a fence around her square garden. She plans to put 8 posts along each side. The diameter of each post is 6 inches. How many posts will there be? _____

7. Alain, Betina, Coley, and Dimitri are artists. One is a potter, one a painter, one a pianist, and one a songwriter. Alain, and Coley saw the pianist perform. Betina and Coley have modeled for the painter. The writer wrote a song about Alain and Dimitri. Bettina is the potter. Who is the songwriter?

   _____

8. Luis is reading a book with 520 pages. When he has read 4 times as many pages as he already has, he will be 184 pages from the end. How many pages has Luis read?

   _____

Practice 4-6 Using Graphs of Equations

Use the graph at the right for Exercises 1–5.

1. What earnings will produce $225 in savings?

   _____

2. How much is saved from earnings of $400?

   _____

3. What is the slope of the line in the graph?

   _____

4. For each increase of $200 in earnings, what is the increase in savings? _____

5. Write an equation for the line.

   _____

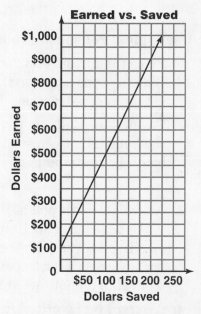

6. A ride in Speedy Cab costs $.40 plus $0.15 per mile.

   a. Write and graph an equation for traveling x miles with Speedy Cab. _____

   b. Speedy Cab charges $0.70 for a ride of how many miles? _____

   c. How much does Speedy Cab charge for a trip of 8 miles? _____

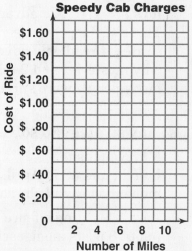

Graph each equation by finding the
x- and y-intercepts.

7. $2x + 3y = 6$

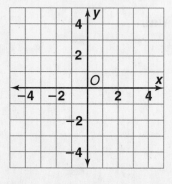

8. $x - 2y = 4$

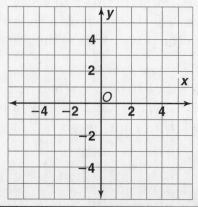

9. $2x - y = -4$

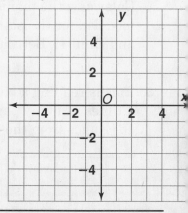

Practice 4-7 *Working with Two Equations*

Here are the graphs of the expense and
income equations for a gift-card sale at a
variety store. Use the graphs for Exercises 1–7.

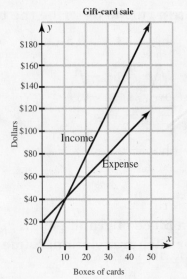

Gift-card sale

1. Suppose the store sells 5 boxes.
   Will there be a profit or a loss? _____

2. How many boxes of cards must
   the store sell in order to break even? _____

3. What are the coordinates of the
   break-even point? _____

4. Suppose the store sells 40 boxes of
   cards. What is the profit? _____

5. Suppose the store makes a profit of
   $80. How many boxes did it sell? _____

6. **a.** Write an equation to represent the income shown on the
   graph. _____

   b. What is the slope and the y-intercept? _____

7. **a.** Write an equation to represent the expenses shown on the
   graph. _____

   b. What is the slope and the y-intercept? _____

8. Kayla sells floral arrangements. The cost of running her
   business is $500 plus $5 per arrangement. She sells her
   arrangements for $25 each. Write and graph equations to
   represent income and expenses. Find the break-even point.

   _____

Expenses for a class party are $200 for music and $5 per
person for food. The class plans to sell tickets for $10 each.
Use this information for Exercises 9–11.

9. Write and graph equations to represent income and expenses.

   _____

10. Use your graph to tell how many tickets must be sold in order
    for the class to break even. _____

11. How many tickets must be sold in order for the class to earn a
    $200 profit? _____

Practice 4-8 Translations

Write a rule to describe the translation shown on each graph.

1.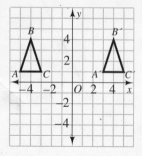

2.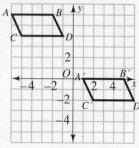

3.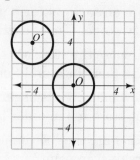

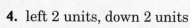

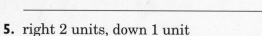

On a piece of graph paper, graph the image of △MNP after each translation. Name the coordinates of M', N', and P'.

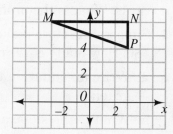

4. left 2 units, down 2 units

   _____

5. right 2 units, down 1 unit

   _____

6. left 2 units, up 3 units

   _____

For Exercises 7–9, draw on a piece of graph paper the image of ☐RSTU after each translation. Name the coordinates of R', S', T', and U'.

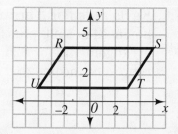

7. right 1 unit, down 2 units

   _____

8. left 3 units, up 0 units

   _____

9. right 2 units, up 4 units

   _____

10. A rectangle has its vertices at M(1, 1), N(6, 1), O(6, 5), and P(1, 5). The rectangle is translated to the left 4 units and down 3 units. What are the coordinates of M', N', O', and P'? Graph the rectangles MNOP and M'N'O'P'.

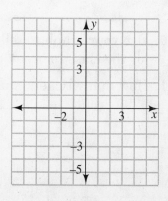

    _____

11. Describe the translation of M'N'O'P' to MNOP.

    _____

Practice 4-9 Reflections and Symmetry

How many lines of symmetry can you find for each letter?

1. W _____   2. X _____   3. H _____   4. T _____

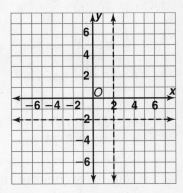

Graph the given point and its image after each reflection. Name the coordinates of the image.

5. $A(5, -4)$ over the vertical dashed line

_____

6. $B(-3, 2)$ over the horizontal dashed line

_____

7. $C(-5, 0)$ over the y-axis

_____

8. $D(3, 4)$ over the x-axis

_____

$\triangle ABC$ **has vertices** $A(2, 1)$, $B(3, -5)$, **and** $C(-2, 4)$**. Graph** $\triangle ABC$ **and its image** $\triangle A'B'C'$ **after a reflection over each line. Name the coordinates of** A', B', **and** C'**.**

9. the x-axis

10. the line through $(-1, 2)$ and $(1, 2)$

11. the y-axis

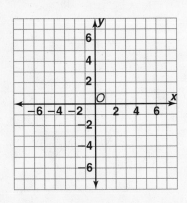

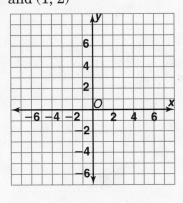

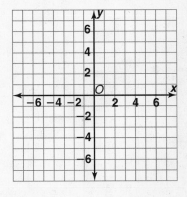

_____

_____

_____

Fold your paper over each dashed line. Are the figures reflections of each other over the given line?

12.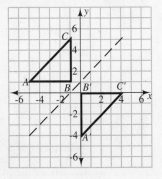

13.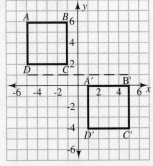

14.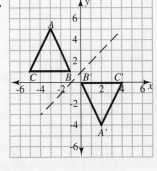

_____   _____   _____

Practice 4-10 Exploring Rotations

Graph each point. Then rotate it the given number of degrees about the origin. Give the coordinates of the image.

1. $V(2, -3)$; 90° _____

2. $M(-4, 5)$; 270° _____

3. $V(0, 5)$; 180° _____

4. $M(6, 0)$; 90° _____

5. $V(3, 4)$; 360° _____

6. $M(0, -1)$; 90° _____

7. Graph $\triangle RST$ with vertices $R(-1, 3)$, $S(4, -2)$, and $T(2, -5)$. Draw the image $\triangle R'S'T'$, formed by rotating $\triangle RST$ 90°, 180°, and 270° about the origin. Give the coordinates of R', S', and T'.

90° _____

180° _____

270° _____

Determine if each figure could be a rotation of the figure at the right. For each figure that could be a rotation, tell what the angle of rotation appears to be.

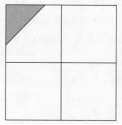

8.

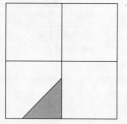

_____

9.

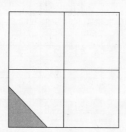

_____

10.

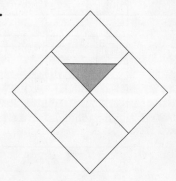

11.

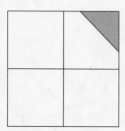

_____

12.

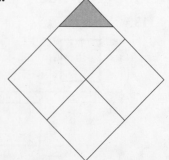

_____

13.

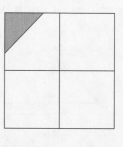

_____

Practice 5-1 Factors

List all the factors of each number.

1. 36 _____   2. 42 _____   3. 50 _____   4. 41 _____

Tell whether the first number is a factor of the second.

5. 2; 71 _____   6. 1; 18 _____   7. 3; 81 _____   8. 4; 74 _____

9. 9; 522 _____   10. 8; 508 _____   11. 13; 179 _____   12. 17; 3,587 _____

Tell whether each number is *prime* or *composite*. If the number is *composite*, list its factors.

13. 74   14. 83   15. 23   16. 51

17. 73   18. 91   19. 109   20. 211

Write the prime factorization of each number.

21. 70   22. 92   23. 120   24. 118

25. 200   26. 180   27. 360   28. 500

29. 187   30. 364   31. 1,287   32. 1,122

Find the GCF of each set of numbers.

33. 24, 40   34. 20, 42   35. 56, 63   36. 48, 72

37. 18, 24, 36   38. 20, 45, 75   39. 120, 150, 180   40. 200, 250, 400

41. Mr. Turner distributed some supplies in his office. He distributed 120 pencils, 300 paper clips, and 16 pens. What is the greatest number of people there can be in the office if each person received the same number of items? _____

42. The baseball league bought new equipment for the teams. The managers bought 288 baseballs, 40 bats, and 24 equipment bags. How many teams are there if all the new equipment is distributed equally among the teams? _____

Practice 5-2 Rational Numbers

Write each rational number as a ratio in the form $\frac{a}{b}$.

1. -5 _____   **2.** 0.63 _____   **3.** -3.9 _____   **4.** $4\frac{5}{6}$ _____

Write three fractions equal to each rational number.

5. $2\frac{1}{2}$ **6.** $-1\frac{3}{4}$ **7.** $3\frac{5}{8}$ **8.** 2.3

_____   _____   _____   _____

Graph each set of rational numbers on a number line.

9. $-3, \frac{2}{3}, 2.75, -\frac{1}{2}, 1.875, -\frac{3}{4}$ **10.** $\frac{2}{5}, 1.4, -2, 2\frac{1}{4}, -1\frac{1}{2}$

$$\xleftarrow{\qquad \overset{-3}{|} \quad \overset{-2}{|} \quad \overset{-1}{|} \quad \overset{0}{|} \quad \overset{1}{|} \quad \overset{2}{|} \quad \overset{3}{|} \qquad} \qquad \xleftarrow{\qquad \overset{-3}{|} \quad \overset{-2}{|} \quad \overset{-1}{|} \quad \overset{0}{|} \quad \overset{1}{|} \quad \overset{2}{|} \quad \overset{3}{|} \qquad}$$

Write each rational number in simplest $\frac{a}{b}$ form.

11. $\frac{77}{99}$ _____   **12.** $\frac{21}{-56}$ _____   **13.** $-\frac{28}{52}$ _____   **14.** $\frac{195}{105}$ _____

15. $\frac{60}{32}$ _____   **16.** $\frac{68}{85}$ _____   **17.** $\frac{-48}{128}$ _____   **18.** $\frac{99}{36}$ _____

Identify each number using as many names as apply. Choose from *whole number*, *integer*, or *rational number*.

19. -9 **20.** 1.6 **21.** 3 **22.** $-1\frac{1}{4}$

_____   _____   _____   _____

23. Circle A, B, C, or D. Which is *not* equal to $-\frac{7}{5}$?

A. $\frac{-14}{10}$ **B.** -1.4 **C.** $-1\frac{1}{5}$ **D.** $\frac{21}{-15}$

Solve.

24. The eighth grade held a magazine sale to raise money for their spring trip. They wanted each student to sell subscriptions. After the first day of the sale, 25 students turned in subscription orders out of 125 eighth graders. Write a rational number in simplest form to express the student response on the first day.

_____

25. Pete wanted to win the prize for selling the most subscriptions. Out of 240 subscriptions sold, Pete sold 30 subscriptions. Write a rational number in simplest form to express Pete's part of the total sales.

_____

Name _____ Class _____ Date _____

▬▬ *Practice 5-3* Equivalent Fractions and Decimals

Choose a calculator, paper and pencil, or mental math. Write each fraction or mixed number as a decimal.

1. $\frac{7}{20}$ _____

2. $-\frac{9}{20}$ _____

3. $-\frac{2}{3}$ _____

4. $1\frac{6}{7}$ _____

5. $3\frac{1}{6}$ _____

6. $-4\frac{7}{8}$ _____

7. $3\frac{11}{12}$ _____

8. $5\frac{7}{11}$ _____

9. $-4\frac{7}{10}$ _____

10. $3\frac{1}{18}$ _____

11. $-1\frac{7}{18}$ _____

12. $2\frac{5}{12}$ _____

13. $-2\frac{7}{9}$ _____

14. $5\frac{7}{15}$ _____

15. $-4\frac{14}{15}$ _____

16. $3\frac{8}{11}$ _____

Write each decimal as a fraction or mixed number in simplest form.

17. 0.006 _____

18. $-4.\overline{8}$ _____

19. 0.97 _____

20. $0.\overline{53}$ _____

21. $0.\overline{4}$ _____

22. 9.05 _____

23. -0.28 _____

24. $5.6\overline{18}$ _____

25. 3.082 _____

26. $-1.\overline{41}$ _____

27. $4.2\overline{3}$ _____

28. $17.\overline{3}$ _____

29. $8.0\overline{5}$ _____

30. $-3.0\overline{2}$ _____

31. $7.1\overline{3}$ _____

32. $4.2\overline{6}$ _____

Use the graph at the right. Write a fraction in simplest form to represent the portion of displaced workers in each age category.

33. 20–24 _____

34. 25–54 _____

35. 55–64 _____

36. 65 and older _____

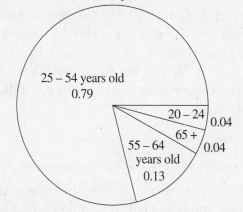

Displaced Workers by Age January 1998

25 – 54 years old
0.79

20 – 24
0.04

65 +
0.04

55 – 64 years old
0.13

Practice 5-4 Comparing and Ordering Rational Numbers

Find the LCM of each pair of numbers.

1. 3, 5 _____   **2.** 2, 6 _____   **3.** 5, 7 _____   **4.** 8, 12 _____

5. 9, 15 _____   **6.** 8, 20 _____   **7.** 6, 20 _____   **8.** 15, 25 _____

9. 28, 40 _____   **10.** 56, 60 _____   **11.** 225, 250 _____   **12.** 180, 150 _____

13. 12, 16 _____   **14.** 15, 24 _____   **15.** 20, 36 _____   **16.** 27, 45 _____

Compare. Use >, <, or =.

17. $-\frac{4}{9}$ ☐ $-\frac{5}{8}$ **18.** $\frac{1}{3}$ ☐ $\frac{6}{18}$ **19.** $\frac{5}{7}$ ☐ 0.63   **20.** -0.76 ☐ $-\frac{3}{4}$

21. $-1\frac{9}{12}$ ☐ $-1\frac{15}{20}$ **22.** $\frac{6}{11}$ ☐ $\frac{5}{9}$ **23.** $\frac{7}{12}$ ☐ 0.59   **24.** $\frac{6}{13}$ ☐ 0.45

Circle A, B, C, or D. Which set of rational numbers is ordered from greatest to least?

25. **A.** $0.74, \frac{3}{4}, \frac{6}{7}, 0.64$ **B.** $\frac{16}{32}, 0.45, \frac{2}{5}, \frac{9}{25}$

    C. $\frac{7}{8}, -\frac{5}{8}, \frac{15}{30}, -\frac{8}{11}$ **D.** $\frac{14}{15}, 0.743, -0.65, \frac{14}{31}$

26. **A.** $\frac{17}{28}, 0.95, \frac{11}{15}, \frac{17}{30}$ **B.** $0.8, 0.5, \frac{5}{8}, \frac{3}{8}$

    C. $\frac{7}{10}, \frac{1}{2}, -0.3, -\frac{3}{4}$ **D.** $-\frac{9}{10}, -\frac{4}{5}, -\frac{1}{2}, -\frac{17}{18}$

27. Parents of Midtown School students are planning a graduation picnic for 117 students. Hot dogs come in packages of 10. Hot dog buns come in packages of 8. Fruit juice comes in packages of 6 cans. How many packages of each item must the parents buy in order to be able to offer a hot dog, bun, and juice to each student?

_____

_____

28. Chris's aunt is giving him a birthday party. She wants to give the same number of balloons, puzzles, and baseball cards to Chris and each guest. Balloons come in packages of 10, puzzles in packs of 8, and baseball cards in packs of 5. There are 7 guests.

    a. How many packages of each item should Chris's aunt buy so that no items are left over?

    _____

    _____

    b. How many of each item will each child receive? _____

Practice 5-5 Adding and Subtracting Like Fractions

Find each sum or difference. Write each answer as a fraction or mixed number in simplest form.

1. $\frac{5}{9} + \frac{7}{9}$

2. $\frac{5}{12} + \left(-\frac{11}{12}\right)$

3. $\frac{11}{20} + \left(-\frac{3}{20}\right)$

4. $-\frac{9}{10} - \frac{3}{10}$

_____ _____ _____ _____

5. $-\frac{2}{5} - \frac{3}{5}$

6. $-\frac{7}{8} - \frac{3}{8}$

7. $\frac{13}{16} - \left(-\frac{15}{16}\right)$

8. $\frac{1}{6} - \left(-\frac{5}{6}\right)$

_____ _____ _____ _____

9. $\frac{3}{10} - \frac{9}{10}$

10. $\frac{8}{9} + \left(-\frac{5}{9}\right)$

11. $-\frac{9}{20} - \frac{3}{20}$

12. $\frac{5}{12} - \frac{7}{12}$

_____ _____ _____ _____

13. $-3\frac{2}{9} - 5\frac{7}{9}$

14. $-6\frac{2}{3} + 1\frac{1}{3}$

15. $2\frac{1}{4} - 5\frac{3}{4}$

_____ _____ _____

16. $-4\frac{1}{8} - \left(-2\frac{5}{8}\right)$

17. $-5\frac{3}{10} + \left(-1\frac{7}{10}\right)$

18. $-3 + \left(-2\frac{19}{30}\right)$

_____ _____ _____

19. $-8\frac{8}{12} + \left(-3\frac{1}{12}\right)$

20. $-4\frac{1}{6} - 5\frac{3}{6}$

21. $7\frac{7}{20} + \left(\frac{8}{20}\right)$

_____ _____ _____

22. $-4\frac{1}{5} - \left(-3\frac{1}{5}\right)$

23. $2\frac{1}{6} - \left(-4\frac{2}{6}\right)$

24. $2\frac{3}{12} + \left(-1\frac{9}{12}\right)$

_____ _____ _____

25. $-3\frac{3}{6} + 2\frac{5}{6}$

26. $-2\frac{6}{9} - \left(-5\frac{4}{9}\right)$

27. $-3\frac{5}{7} - 4\frac{4}{7}$

_____ _____ _____

Solve.

28. The school band practiced for $2\frac{3}{4}$ hours on Saturday and $1\frac{1}{4}$ hours on Sunday. How many hours did they practice in all?

_____

29. Maria ran $1\frac{1}{10}$ miles and walked $\frac{7}{10}$ mile. How far did she travel in all?

_____

Practice 5-6 Adding and Subtracting Rational Numbers

Write each sum or difference as a fraction or mixed number in simplest form.

1. $\frac{3}{4} + \frac{7}{8}$ _____

2. $-1\frac{1}{6} + 2\frac{2}{3}$ _____

3. $4\frac{1}{2} - 7\frac{7}{8}$ _____

4. $-3\frac{5}{6} - \left(-4\frac{1}{12}\right)$ _____

5. $\frac{5}{18} + \frac{7}{12}$ _____

6. $-4\frac{7}{20} + 3\frac{9}{10}$ _____

7. $5\frac{8}{21} - \left(-3\frac{1}{7}\right)$ _____

8. $1\frac{19}{24} + 2\frac{23}{20}$ _____

9. $3\frac{16}{25} - 4\frac{7}{20}$ _____

10. $5\frac{1}{14} + 2\frac{3}{7} + 1\frac{4}{21}$ _____

11. $\frac{11}{12} - \frac{5}{16} + \frac{11}{18}$ _____

12. $\frac{5}{6} + \frac{7}{8} - \frac{11}{12}$ _____

13. $-19\frac{5}{6} + 10\frac{9}{10}$ _____

14. $4\frac{7}{18} - 3\frac{7}{12}$ _____

15. $-1\frac{4}{5} - \left(-4\frac{1}{12}\right)$ _____

Write each answer as a fraction or mixed number in simplest form. Then rewrite as a decimal.

16. $14.6 + \left(-3\frac{1}{5}\right)$

17. $-7\frac{3}{4} - 4.125$

18. $5.75 + \left(-2\frac{1}{8}\right)$

_____   _____   _____

19. $1\frac{3}{4} - 2.75 - 4\frac{5}{8}$

20. $3\frac{1}{2} - 6\frac{7}{10} + 4\frac{1}{5}$

21. $\frac{3}{16} + \frac{1}{8} - \frac{1}{4}$

_____   _____   _____

Solve each equation.

22. $x + \frac{3}{8} = -\frac{1}{4}$

23. $y - \frac{1}{5} = -\frac{4}{5}$

24. $z + \left(-\frac{2}{3}\right) = -\frac{1}{6}$

_____   _____   _____

25. $m - \frac{9}{10} = \frac{1}{5}$

26. $n - 1\frac{1}{3} = -3$

27. $p + \frac{7}{12} = -\frac{1}{4}$

_____   _____   _____

28. $c - 7.2 = -3.7$

29. $d - 0.16 = 2.3$

30. $\frac{1}{8} + a = -2\frac{1}{4}$

_____   _____   _____

31. Stanley is helping in the library by mending torn pages. He has
cut strips of tape with lengths of $5\frac{1}{2}$ in., $6\frac{7}{8}$ in., $3\frac{3}{4}$ in., and $4\frac{3}{16}$ in.
What is the total length of tape he has used?

_____

Practice 5-7 Multiplying and Dividing Rational Numbers

Choose a calculator, paper and pencil, or mental math to find each product or quotient.

1. $-\frac{1}{6} \cdot 2\frac{3}{4}$ _____

2. $\frac{3}{16} \div (-\frac{1}{8})$ _____

3. $-\frac{31}{56} \cdot (-8)$ _____

4. $-5\frac{7}{12} \div 12$ _____

5. $-8 \div \frac{1}{4}$ _____

6. $-3\frac{1}{6} \div \left(-2\frac{1}{12}\right)$ _____

7. $8\frac{3}{4} \cdot 3\frac{7}{8}$ _____

8. $-\frac{11}{12} \div \frac{5}{6}$ _____

9. $4\frac{9}{28} \cdot (-7)$ _____

10. $-1\frac{1}{15} \div 15$ _____

11. $-3 \div \frac{3}{4}$ _____

12. $-2\frac{7}{8} \div 3\frac{3}{4}$ _____

13. $-\frac{23}{24} \cdot (-8)$ _____

14. $\frac{7}{8} \cdot \left(-\frac{2}{7}\right)$ _____

15. $-7 \div \frac{1}{9}$ _____

16. $-6\frac{5}{6} \div \frac{1}{6}$ _____

17. $-8 \cdot 3\frac{3}{4}$ _____

18. $\frac{7}{10} \cdot \left(-3\frac{1}{4}\right)$ _____

19. $5 \cdot \left(-3\frac{5}{6}\right)$ _____

20. $-\frac{8}{9} \div \left(-3\frac{2}{3}\right)$ _____

21. $2\frac{1}{3} \div \frac{2}{3}$ _____

Solve each equation.

22. $\frac{1}{3}a = \frac{3}{10}$

23. $-\frac{3}{4}b = 9$

24. $-\frac{7}{8}c = 4\frac{2}{3}$

_____

_____

_____

25. $\frac{5}{6}n = -3\frac{3}{4}$

26. $-\frac{3}{5}x = 12$

27. $-2\frac{2}{3}y = 3\frac{1}{3}$

_____

_____

_____

28. $\frac{7}{12}y = -2\frac{4}{5}$

29. $2\frac{1}{4}z = -\frac{1}{9}$

30. $2\frac{1}{5}d = -\frac{1}{2}$

_____

_____

_____

31. One pound of flour contains about four cups. A recipe calls for $2\frac{1}{4}$ c of flour. How many full recipes can you make from a two-pound bag of flour? _____

32. Kim needs $2\frac{1}{2}$ ft of wrapping paper to wrap each package. She has five packages to wrap. How many packages can she wrap with a 12-ft roll of wrapping paper? _____

33. Gina and Paul are making pizza for the cast and crew of the school play. They estimate that the boys in the cast and crew will eat $\frac{1}{2}$ pizza each. They estimate that the girls will each eat $\frac{1}{3}$ of a pizza. There are 7 boys and 10 girls working on the play. How many pizzas do they need to make? _____

Practice 5-8 Problem-Solving Strategy: Work Backward

Work backward to solve each problem.

1. Alli withdrew some money from the bank for shopping. She spent two thirds of what she withdrew on groceries. She spent $25 on a sweater. She spent half of what remained on a necklace. She went home with $15. How much did Alli withdraw from the bank? _____

2. Jill met her friends at the movies at 2 P.M. on Saturday after washing windows. It took her $\frac{3}{4}$ h to wash the windows at the first house. It took twice as long to wash the windows at the next house. The last house took $1\frac{1}{2}$ h. After that, it took her $\frac{1}{2}$ h to walk to the movie theater. At what time did Jill start washing windows? _____

3. If you start with a number, add 4, multiply by 3, subtract 10, then divide by 4, the result is 5. What is the number? _____

4. Phil had a busy day with his tow truck. He didn't return to the garage until 4:00 P.M. It took $1\frac{3}{4}$ h to get the car back to the garage from the last call. The call before that took Phil twice as long. He took a half hour for lunch. One call in the morning took Phil only a half hour, but the one before that took five times as long. What time did Phil's work day begin? _____

5. A ball is bouncing on the floor. After each bounce, the height of the ball is one-half its previous height. After the fifth bounce, the height of the ball is 6 in. What was the height of the ball before the first bounce? _____

6. If you start with a number, subtract 4, multiply by $\frac{1}{4}$, add 6, then divide by 2, the result is 10. What is the number? _____

7. Matt spent $\frac{1}{5}$ of his money on a concert ticket. He spent $60 on a new jacket and $2.50 for bus fare. He reached home with $17.50. How much did he have to begin with? _____

8. Bob sells planters at craft shows. At the first craft show, he sold a fourth of his planters. At the next craft show, he sold 14 more. At the third he sold half of what remained. At the fourth show he sold the remaining 20. How many planters did Bob sell?

_____

Practice 5-9 *Exploring Square Roots and Irrational Numbers*

Find each square root. If a number is not a perfect square, approximate the square root to the nearest tenth.

1. $\sqrt{81}$

2. $\sqrt{76}$

3. $\sqrt{121}$

4. $\sqrt{289}$

5. $\sqrt{130}$

6. $\sqrt{8}$

7. $\sqrt{144}$

8. $\sqrt{160}$

9. $\sqrt{182}$

10. $\sqrt{256}$

11. $\sqrt{301}$

12. $\sqrt{350}$

13. $\sqrt{361}$

14. $\sqrt{410}$

15. $\sqrt{441}$

16. $\sqrt{500}$

Identify each number as rational or irrational.

17. $\sqrt{16}$

18. $\sqrt{11}$

19. $\sqrt{196}$

20. $\sqrt{200}$

21. $\sqrt{1,521}$

22. $\sqrt{785}$

23. $\sqrt{529}$

24. $\sqrt{1,680}$

25. $\sqrt{2,000}$

26. $\sqrt{3,969}$

27. $\sqrt{3,192}$

28. $\sqrt{15,376}$

For each number, write all the categories to which it belongs. Choose from *real number*, *rational number*, *irrational number*, *integer*, and *whole number*.

29. $\frac{4}{5}$ _____

30. $0.7\overline{12}$ _____

31. -8 _____

32. $\sqrt{3}$ _____

33. 5.2 _____

34. 52 _____

35. $-\sqrt{25}$ _____

36. $\sqrt{306}$ _____

37. 2.7064 _____

38. $-\sqrt{121}$ _____

39. 0 _____

40. $\sqrt{12}$ _____

Use a calculator. Find each product.

41. $\sqrt{5} \cdot \sqrt{3}$ _____

42. $\sqrt{4} \cdot \sqrt{5}$ _____

43. $\sqrt{3} \cdot \sqrt{3}$ _____

44. $\sqrt{5} \cdot \sqrt{245}$ _____

45. $\sqrt{3} \cdot \sqrt{21}$ _____

46. $\sqrt{8} \cdot \sqrt{50}$ _____

Practice 5-10 The Pythagorean Theorem

Find the missing side length to the nearest tenth.

1.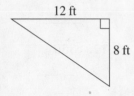

17 cm

15 cm

_____

2.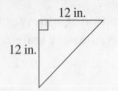

12 in.

12 in.

_____

3.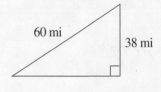

9 m

12 m

_____

4. 12 ft

8 ft

_____

5.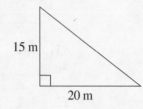

15 m

20 m

_____

6.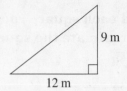

60 mi

38 mi

_____

Is a triangle with the given side lengths a right triangle?

7. 8 cm, 12 cm, 15 cm

_____

8. 9 in., 12 in., 15 in.

_____

9. 5 m, 12 m, 25 m

_____

10. 15 in., 36 in., 39 in.

_____

11. 10 m, 20 m, 25 m

_____

12. 7 mm, 24 mm, 25 mm

_____

13. 9 yd, 40 yd, 41 yd

_____

14. 10 cm, 25 cm, 26 cm

_____

15. 27 yd, 120 yd, 130 yd

_____

16. 11 mi, 60 mi, 61 mi

_____

You are given three circles, as shown. Points *A, B, C, D, E, F,* and *G* lie on the same line. Find each length to the nearest tenth.

17. *HD* _____   **18.** *IE* _____   **19.** *JD* _____

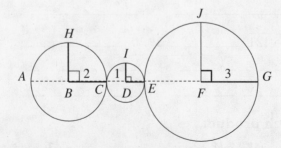

Practice 6-1 Exploring Ratios and Rates

Write three ratios that each model can represent.

1.

_____

_____

_____

2.

_____

_____

_____

3.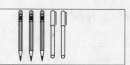

_____

_____

_____

Write each ratio in simplest form.

4. $9:12$

_____

5. 20 out of 25

_____

6. 16 to 24

_____

7. $\frac{6}{21}$

_____

8. 100 to 85

_____

9. $\frac{18}{30}$

_____

10. 6 in. to 2 ft

_____

11. 10 min to 3 h

_____

12. 20 s to 5 min

_____

Write the unit rate.

13. $67.92 for 4 gal

_____

14. $21.00 for 6 h

_____

15. 250 mi in 4 h

_____

16. 141 words in 3 min

_____

17. $5.94 for 6 carnations

_____

18. 36 min for 12 songs

_____

**The table at the right shows the results of a survey. Write
each ratio in simplest form and as a decimal rounded to the
nearest hundredth.**

Which Meal Do You Want for the Party?	
Tacos	Pizza

19. *Tacos* to *Pizza*

_____

20. *Pizza* to *Tacos*

_____

21. *Tacos* to the total

_____

22. *Pizza* to the total

_____

23. Which is the better buy: a 16-oz box of
cereal for $3.89 or a 6-oz box of cereal
for $1.55?

_____

24. A bag contains 8 yellow marbles and 6
blue marbles. What number of yellow
marbles can you add to the bag so that
the ratio of yellow to blue marbles is 2 : 1?

_____

Practice 6-2 Units of Measurement

What customary unit would you use for each measure?

1. length of a stapler

2. weight of a cookie

3. capacity of a teakettle

_____

_____

_____

4. height of a door

5. distance to the moon

6. weight of a jet aircraft

_____

_____

_____

What metric unit would you use for each measure?

7. mass of a cat

8. length of a playground

9. capacity of a test tube

_____

_____

_____

10. length of an insect

11. capacity of a bathtub

12. mass of a coin

_____

_____

_____

Use dimensional analysis to convert each measure. Round answers to the nearest hundredth where necessary.

13. 56 in. = ▇ ft

14. 240 d = ▇ h

15. 4 gal = ▇ pt

_____

_____

_____

16. 0.75 d = ▇ h

17. 2.25 t = ▇ lb

18. 84 ft = ▇ yd

_____

_____

_____

19. 0.25 d = ▇ min

20. 18 d = ▇ h

21. 0.01 t = ▇ oz

_____

_____

_____

Use dimensional analysis to solve each problem.

22. At one time, trains were not permitted to go faster than 12 mi/h. How many yards per minute is this?

_____

23. A mosquito can fly at 0.6 mi/h. How many inches per second is this?

_____

24. An Arctic tern flew 11,000 miles in 115 days. How many feet per minute did the bird average?

_____

25. A sneeze can travel up to 100 mi/h. How many feet per second is this?

_____

Practice 6-3 Solving Proportions

Solve each proportion using mental math.

1. $\frac{3}{8} = \frac{m}{16}$ _____

2. $\frac{9}{4} = \frac{27}{x}$ _____

3. $\frac{18}{6} = \frac{j}{1}$ _____

4. $\frac{b}{18} = \frac{7}{6}$ _____

5. $\frac{12}{q} = \frac{3}{4}$ _____

6. $\frac{3}{2} = \frac{15}{r}$ _____

7. $\frac{5}{x} = \frac{25}{15}$ _____

8. $\frac{80}{20} = \frac{4}{n}$ _____

Estimate the solution of each proportion.

9. $\frac{m}{25} = \frac{16}{98}$ _____

10. $\frac{7}{3} = \frac{52}{n}$ _____

11. $\frac{30}{5.9} = \frac{k}{10}$ _____

12. $\frac{2.8}{j} = \frac{1.3}{2.71}$ _____

13. $\frac{y}{12} = \frac{2.89}{4.23}$ _____

14. $\frac{5}{8} = \frac{b}{63}$ _____

15. $\frac{9}{4} = \frac{35}{d}$ _____

16. $\frac{c}{7} = \frac{28}{50}$ _____

Choose a calculator, paper and pencil, or mental math to solve each proportion.

17. $\frac{4}{5} = \frac{b}{40}$

18. $\frac{11}{7} = \frac{88}{c}$

19. $\frac{x}{1.4} = \frac{28}{5.6}$

20. $\frac{0.99}{a} = \frac{9}{11}$

_____

_____

_____

_____

21. $\frac{42.5}{20} = \frac{x}{8}$

22. $\frac{15}{25} = \frac{7.5}{y}$

23. $\frac{16}{b} = \frac{56}{38.5}$

24. $\frac{z}{54} = \frac{5}{12}$

_____

_____

_____

_____

25. $\frac{8}{12} = \frac{e}{3}$

26. $\frac{v}{35} = \frac{15}{14}$

27. $\frac{60}{n} = \frac{12}{5}$

28. $\frac{6}{16} = \frac{9}{w}$

_____

_____

_____

_____

29. $\frac{4}{7} = \frac{r}{35}$

30. $\frac{18}{16} = \frac{27}{t}$

31. $\frac{n}{12} = \frac{12.5}{15}$

32. $\frac{27}{f} = \frac{40.5}{31.5}$

_____

_____

_____

_____

33. 5 is to 8 as 15 is to w

34. y is to 8 as 22.5 is to 10

35. 14 is to b as 28 is to 18

_____

_____

_____

36. 10 is to 7 as m is to 10.5

37. 30 is to 16 as j is to 8

38. r is to 17 as 81 is to 51

_____

_____

_____

Write a proportion for each situation. Then solve.

39. Jaime paid $1.29 for three ponytail holders. At that rate, what would eight ponytail holders cost her?

40. According to a label, there are 25 calories per serving of turkey lunch meat. How many calories are there in 2.5 servings?

_____

_____

41. Arturo paid $8.00 in tax on a purchase of $200.00. At that rate, what would the tax be on a purchase of $150.00?

42. Chris drove 200 mi in 4 h. At that rate, how long would it take Chris to drive 340 mi?

_____

_____

Practice 6-4 Similar Figures and Proportions

Tell whether each figure shows a pair of similar polygons. If so, state the similarity.

1.
B ──8── C F ─4─ G
12   6
A   D E   H

_____

2.

_____

3.
T
9   11
S ──8── U

_____

4.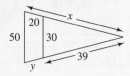

_____

5.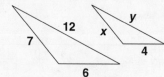

_____

6.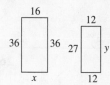

_____

Each figure shows a pair of similar polygons. Find each unknown length.

7.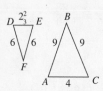

_____

8.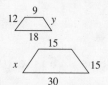

_____

9.
16
36   36   12
x   27   y
            12

_____

10.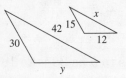

_____

11.
12 ─9─ y
18   15
x   15
  30

_____

12.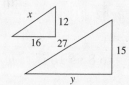

_____

Solve.

13. A rock show is being televised. The lead singer, who is 75 inches tall, is 15 inches tall on a TV monitor. The image of the bass player is 13 inches tall on the monitor. How tall is the bass player?

_____

14. A 42-inch-long guitar is 10.5-feet-long on a stadium screen. A drum is 21 inches wide. How wide is the image on the stadium screen?

_____

▰▰▰ *Practice 6-5* Similarity Transformations

**Graph quadrilateral *ABCD* and its image *A′B′C′D′*
after a dilation with center (0, 0) and the given
scale factor.**

1. $A(2, -2), B(3, 2), C(-3, 2), D(-2, -2)$;
   scale factor 2

2. $A(6, 3), B(0, 6), C(-6, 2), D(-6, -5)$;
   scale factor $\frac{1}{2}$

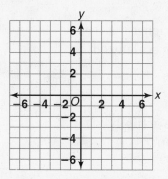

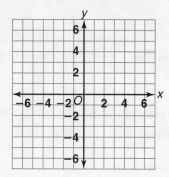

**Quadrilateral *A′B′C′D′* is a dilation of
quadrilateral *ABCD*. Find the scale factor and
classify each dilation as an enlargement or a
reduction.**

3.

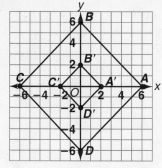

4.

5.

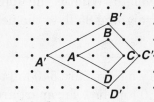

_____   _____   _____

6. A triangle has coordinates $A(-2, -2), B(4, -2)$, and $C(1, 1)$. Its
   image after a dilation with center (0, 0) and scale factor $\frac{3}{2}$ is
   figure $A′B′C′$. Give the coordinates of $A′B′C′$, and the ratio of
   the areas of the figures $A′B′C′$ and ABC.

_____

Practice 6-6 *Using Proportions to Solve Problems*

Use a proportion to solve each problem. Show all your work.

1. A scale model of a whale is being built. The actual length of the whale is 65 ft. The scale of the model is 2 in. : 3 ft. What will be the length of the model?

    _____

2. The smallest frog known is only $\frac{1}{2}$ in. long. A local science museum is planning to build a model of the frog. The scale used will be 3 in. : $\frac{1}{4}$ in. How long will the model be?

    _____

3. Two cities on a map were $2\frac{1}{4}$ in. apart. The cities are actually 56.25 mi apart. What scale was used to draw the map?

    _____

4. Four ounces of a certain perfume cost $20.96. How much would six ounces of perfume cost?

    _____

5. The human brain weighs about 1 lb for each 100 lb of body weight. What is the approximate weight of the brain of a person weighing 85 lb to the nearest ounce?

    _____

6. Two towns are 540 km apart. If the scale on the map is 2 cm to 50 km, how far apart are the towns on the map?

    _____

7. Cans of tuna cost $1.59 for $6\frac{1}{2}$ oz. At that rate, how much would 25 oz of tuna cost?

    _____

8. Students are building a model of a volcano. The volcano is about 8,000 ft tall. The students want the model to be 18 in. tall. What scale should they use?

    _____

9. A certain shade of paint requires 3 parts of blue to 2 parts of yellow to 1 part of red. If 18 gal of that shade of paint are needed, how many gal of blue are needed?

    _____

▰▰▰ *Practice 6-7* *Problem-Solving Strategy:*
Draw a Diagram

Use diagrams to solve each problem.

1. A Super Bounce Ball is dropped from a height of 64 ft. With each bounce, the ball reaches a height that is three-fourths the height of the previous bounce. After how many bounces will the ball bounce up to a height less than 9 in.?

   _____

2. Mr. Flanders directs a package delivery route. His first stop is 6 mi east of his house. He then proceeds 4 mi south to his next stop. His third stop is 3 mi west of the second stop. He then travels 2 mi south and 3 mi west. At this point, how far is Mr. Flanders from his house?

   _____

3. Fourteen minivans, each holding the same number of students and one driver, set out for the spring track competition. On the way, 2 minivans broke down and were towed away for repair. Each of the remaining minivans took on one additional person, and they continued on to the competition. How many people in all went to the competition in this group?

   _____

4. Sweeney leaves on a 20-mi bike trip. He rides his bicycle at a speed of 8 mi/h. Shayna leaves 1 h later. Both bikers take the same route. Shayna rides at a speed of 6 mi/h. How much later than Sweeney will Shayna complete the trip?

   _____

Use any strategy to solve each problem. Show your work.

5. Kevin scored 40 out of 100 points on his first math test. If he gets a perfect 100 on all other math tests, how many more tests will it take for him to bring his mean score up to 80?

   _____

6. Veronica started an after-school business of making wreaths. She employs 12 friends who work on the wreaths in 3 steps: cutting fabric into strips; stuffing the strips into the wreaths; and attaching the beads and bows. One person can cut enough fabric for 15 wreaths per day; one person can stuff fabric into 12 wreaths per day; and one person can attach beads and bows to 20 wreaths per day. How many employees should Veronica assign to each step?

   _____

Practice 6-8 *Similarity and Indirect Measurement*

Use the similar triangles to find each unknown distance.

1.
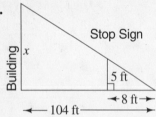

_____

2.
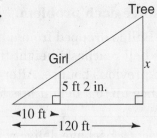

_____

3.
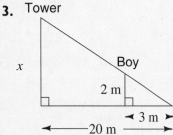

_____

4.
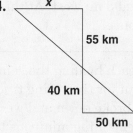

_____

5.
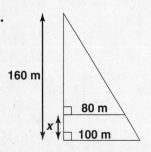

_____

6.
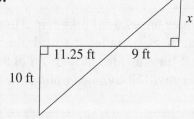

_____

7. An office building 55 ft tall casts a shadow 30 ft long. How tall is a person standing nearby who casts a shadow 3 ft long?

_____

8. A 20-ft pole casts a shadow 12 ft long. How tall is a nearby building that casts a shadow 20 ft long?

_____

9. A fire tower casts a shadow 30 ft long. A nearby tree casts a shadow 8 ft long. How tall is the fire tower if the tree is 20 ft tall?

_____

10. A house casts a shadow 12 m long. A tree in the yard casts a shadow 8 m long. How tall is the tree if the house is 20 m tall?

_____

Practice 6-9 The Tangent Ratio

Refer to △ MNO.

1. Which leg is opposite ∠M?

   _____

2. Which leg is opposite ∠N?

   _____

3. Which leg is adjacent to ∠M?

   _____

4. Which leg is adjacent to ∠N?

   _____

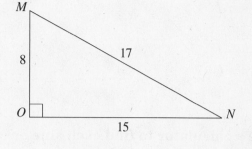

5. Find tan M as a fraction and as a decimal.

   _____

6. Find tan N as a fraction and as a decimal.

   _____

Use a calculator to find each tangent. Round to the nearest ten-thousandth.

7. tan 26° _____ 8. tan 30° _____ 9. tan 47° _____ 10. tan 50° _____

11. tan 8° _____ 12. tan 88° _____ 13. tan 15° _____ 14. tan 65° _____

For each figure, use a calculator to find tan A and tan B. Round to the nearest ten-thousandth.

15.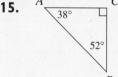

16.

17.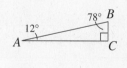

18.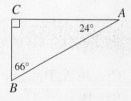

_____ _____ _____ _____

_____ _____ _____ _____

In each figure, find n. Round to the nearest tenth.

19.

20.

21.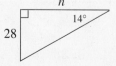

22.

_____ _____ _____ _____

▬▬▬ *Practice 6-10* The Sine and Cosine Ratios

Write each trigonometric ratio as a fraction in simplest form.

1. sin *J*

2. cos *J*

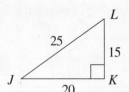

_____

3. sin *L*

4. cos *L*

_____

Use a calculator to find each sine or cosine. Round to the nearest ten-thousandth.

5. sin 48°

6. cos 57°

7. sin 18°

8. cos 18°

_____ _____ _____ _____

9. sin 89°

10. cos 89°

11. sin 37°

12. cos 8°

_____ _____ _____ _____

13. sin 54°

14. cos 62°

15. sin 75°

16. cos 15°

_____ _____ _____ _____

Use the Pythagorean Theorem to find *n*. Then write sin *X*, cos *X*, and tan *X* as fractions in simplest form.

17.

18.

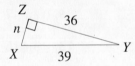

19.

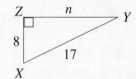

_____ _____ _____

Circle A, B, C, or D. In each triangle, which equation can you use to find *n*?

20.

M, 17, 6, 21°, N, n, O

I. $\sin 21° = \frac{n}{17}$

II. $\cos 21° = \frac{n}{17}$

III. $\tan 21° = \frac{6}{n}$

A. I only

B. II only

C. III only

D. II or III only

21.

M, n, 9, 33°, N, 14, O

I. $\sin 33° = \frac{9}{n}$

II. $\cos 33° = \frac{14}{n}$

III. $\tan 33° = \frac{9}{14}$

A. I only

B. I or II only

C. II or III only

D. I, II, or III

Practice 7-1 Fractions, Decimals, and Percents

Use mental math to write each decimal as a percent.

1. 0.95 _____   **2.** 0.06 _____   **3.** 0.004 _____   **4.** 0.27 _____

5. 0.63 _____   **6.** 0.005 _____   **7.** 1.4 _____   **8.** 2.57 _____

Choose a calculator, paper and pencil, or mental math to write each fraction as a percent. Round to the nearest tenth.

9. $\frac{4}{5}$ _____   **10.** $\frac{7}{10}$ _____   **11.** $\frac{5}{6}$ _____   **12.** $4\frac{1}{2}$ _____

13. $\frac{5}{8}$ _____   **14.** $\frac{1}{15}$ _____   **15.** $\frac{9}{25}$ _____   **16.** $1\frac{7}{8}$ _____

17. $\frac{1}{6}$ _____   **18.** $\frac{11}{12}$ _____   **19.** $\frac{1}{20}$ _____   **20.** $3\frac{9}{20}$ _____

Use mental math to write each percent as a decimal.

21. 70% _____   **22.** 10% _____   **23.** 800% _____   **24.** 37% _____

25. 2.6% _____   **26.** 234% _____   **27.** 9% _____   **28.** $3\frac{1}{2}$% _____

Write each percent as a fraction or mixed number in simplest form.

29. 10% _____   **30.** 47% _____   **31.** $5\frac{1}{2}$% _____   **32.** 473% _____

33. 15% _____   **34.** 92% _____   **35.** $3\frac{1}{4}$% _____   **36.** 548% _____

37. 85% _____   **38.** 42% _____   **39.** 70% _____   **40.** 150% _____

Solve.

41. There are twelve pairs of cranial nerves connected to the brain. Ten of these pairs are related to sight, smell, taste, and sound. What percent of the pairs are related to sight, smell, taste, and sound? _____

42. If a person weighs 150 lb, then calcium makes up 3 lb of that person's weight. What percent of a person's weight does calcium make up?

_____

43. A quality control inspector found that 43 out of every 50 radios produced were not defective. What percent of the radios were not defective?

_____

44. In 1992, 80 varieties of reptiles were on the endangered species list. Eight of these were found only in the United States. What percent of the reptiles on the endangered species list were found only in the United States? _____

Practice 7-2 Estimating with Percents

Estimate the percent of the number using any method.

1. 6% of 140 ____   **2.** 18.9% of 44 ____   **3.** 61% of 180 ____   **4.** 5.1% of 81 ____

5. $16\frac{1}{2}$% of 36 ____   **6.** 81% of 241 ____   **7.** 67% of 300 ____   **8.** 51% of 281 ____

9. 62.9% of 400 ____ **10.** 76% of 600 ____   **11.** 88% of 680 ____   **12.** 37% of 481 ____

13. 19.1% of 380 ____ **14.** 41% of 321 ____   **15.** 33% of 331 ____   **16.** 83% of 453 ____

17. 76.3% of 841 ____ **18.** 67.1% of 486 ____ **19.** 84% of 93 ____   **20.** 0.3% of 849 ____

21. 81.2% of 974 ____ **22.** 0.87% of 250 ____ **23.** 57.9% of 500 ____ **24.** 62% of 400 ____

Circle A, B, C, or D. Estimate each percent.

25. 40% of 603

    A. 24   **B.** 120

    C. 240   **D.** 24,000

26. 21% of 847

    A. 170   **B.** 340

    C. 17   **D.** 17,000

27. 33% of 986

    A. 33   **B.** 330

    C. 660   **D.** 33,000

28. 87% of 559

    A. 350   **B.** 49

    C. 49,000   **D.** 490

Estimate.

29. Of the 307 species of mammals on the endangered list in 1992, 12.1% of them were found only in the United States. Estimate the number of mammal species in the United States that were on the endangered list. _____

30. In 1990, 19% of the people of Mali lived in urban settings. If the population that year was 9,200,000, estimate the number of people who lived in urban settings. _____

31. Of the 1,267 students at the school, 9.8% live within walking distance of school. Estimate the number of students within walking distance.

_____

32. Of the 1,267 students at the school, 54.6% have to ride the bus. About how many students have to ride the bus?

_____

▬▬▬ *Practice 7-3* Percents and Proportions

Circle A, B, C, or D. For each of the following, choose the proportion that will help you answer the question.

1. What percent is 21 of 50?

   A. $\frac{21}{50} = \frac{n}{100}$ **B.** $\frac{n}{50} = \frac{21}{100}$ **C.** $\frac{21}{n} = \frac{100}{50}$ **D.** $\frac{n}{21} = \frac{42}{100}$

2. What is 45% of 72?

   A. $\frac{45}{72} = \frac{n}{100}$ **B.** $\frac{n}{72} = \frac{45}{100}$ **C.** $\frac{45}{72} = \frac{100}{n}$ **D.** $\frac{72}{100} = \frac{45}{n}$

3. 83 is 70% of what number?

   A. $\frac{n}{100} = \frac{70}{83}$ **B.** $\frac{100}{83} = \frac{n}{70}$ **C.** $\frac{83}{100} = \frac{70}{n}$ **D.** $\frac{83}{n} = \frac{70}{100}$

4. 45 is what percent of 65?

   A. $\frac{45}{100} = \frac{65}{n}$ **B.** $\frac{45}{n} = \frac{100}{65}$ **C.** $\frac{45}{65} = \frac{n}{100}$ **D.** $\frac{45}{100} = \frac{n}{65}$

Choose a calculator, paper and pencil, or mental math to solve each of the following. Round to the nearest hundredth.

5. 78% of 58 is _____   6. 86 is 12% of _____   7. 90 is _____ of 65.

8. 40 is 17% of _____   9. 57 is 31% of _____   10. 280% of _____ is 418.

11. 53% of 92 is _____   12. 56 is 25% of _____   13. 51 is _____ of 14.

14. What percent of 42 is 18? _____   15. 58 is 40% of what number? _____

16. What is 70% of 93? _____   17. 240 is what percent of 150? _____

18. What percent of 16 is 40? _____   19. 65 is 60% of what number? _____

20. What is 175% of 48? _____   21. 210 is what percent of 70? _____

22. What percent of 56 is 7? _____   23. 68 is 50% of what number? _____

24. What is 63% of 148? _____   25. 215 is what percent of 400? _____

Solve.

26. In 1990, the population of El Paso, Texas, was 515,342. Of this population, 69% were of Hispanic origin. How many people were of Hispanic origin?

   _____

27. Bangladesh covers 55,598 mi^2. Of this land, 2,224 mi^2 are meadows and pastures. What percent of 55,598 is 2,224?

   _____

▄▄▄ Practice 7-4 Percents and Equations

Use an equation to solve each problem. Round to the nearest tenth.

1. What percent of 80 is 25? _____

2. 8.6 is 5% of what number? _____

3. What is 140% of 85? _____

4. 70 is what percent of 120? _____

5. What percent of 90 is 42? _____

6. 18.4 is what percent of 10? _____

7. 56% of what number is 82? _____

8. Find 93% of 150. _____

9. 30% of what number is 120? _____

10. What percent of 420 is 7? _____

11. 79 is what percent of 250? _____

12. 9.1 is 3% of what number? _____

13. What is 94% of 260? _____

14. 45 is what percent of 18? _____

15. What percent of 280 is 157? _____

16. 20.7 is what percent of 8? _____

17. 114% of what number is 75? _____

18. Find 72% of 18,495. _____

19. 75% of what number is 200? _____

20. What percent of 940 is 15? _____

21. 80 is what percent of 450? _____

22. Find 65% of 2,190. _____

23. 90 is what percent of 40? _____

24. 45 is what percent of 900? _____

25. 82 is 90% of what number? _____

26. 50 is 120% of what number? _____

Solve.

27. In a recent survey, 216 people, or 54% of the sample, said they usually went to a family restaurant when they went out to eat. How many people were surveyed? _____

28. In a school survey, 248 students, or 32% of the sample, said they worked part time during the summer. How many students were in the sample?

_____

29. Juliet sold a house for $112,000. What percent commission did she receive if she earned $6,720?

_____

30. Jason earns $200 per week plus 8% commission on his sales. How much were his sales last week if Jason earned $328?

_____

31. Stella makes 2% royalties on a book she wrote. How much money did her book earn in sales last year if she made $53,000 in royalties? _____

32. Linda earns $40 base pay per week, plus 10% commission on all sales. What were sales if she made $112 in one week?

_____

33. Kevin sold a house for $57,000. His fee, or sale commission, for selling the house was $2,679. What percent of the price of the house was Kevin's commission?

_____

34. Marik agreed to pay a realtor 6.5% commission for selling his house. If the house sold for $68,900, how much does Marik have after paying the realtor's commission? _____

Practice 7-5 Creating Circle Graphs

**The Rahman family has a budget for their summer vacation.
Complete the table below. Use the results to construct a
circle graph.**

	Category	Amount Budgeted	Percent of Total	Degrees in Central Angle
1.	Gas	$200		
2.	Meals	$400		
3.	Motels	$600		
4.	Other	$800		

**Lucy has set up a budget. Complete the table below. Use the
results to construct a circle graph.**

	Category	Amount Budgeted	Percent of Total	Degrees in Central Angle
5.	Clothing	$50		
6.	Entertainment	$40		
7.	Savings	$25		
8.	Transportation	$10		

9. A dairy association surveyed customers to
find out whether they were drinking more
milk than they were a year ago. Here is how
they responded. Display the responses in a
circle graph.

more	56.3%
the same	20.5%
less	10.1%
not sure	13.1%

Name _____ Class _____ Date _____

Practice 7-6 Percent of Change

Find each percent of change. Label your answer as increase or decrease. Round to the nearest tenth of a percent.

1. 15 to 20

2. 18 to 10

3. 10 to 7.5

4. 86 to 120

5. 17 to 34

6. 32 to 24

7. 27 to 38

8. 40 to 10

9. 8 to 10

10. 43 to 86

11. 100 to 23

12. 846 to 240

13. 130 to 275

14. 193 to 270

15. 436 to 118

16. 457 to 318

17. 607 to 812

18. 500 to 118

19. 346 to 843

20. 526 to 1,000

21. 1,000 to 526

22. 489 to 751

23. 286 to 781

24. 846 to 957

Solve.

25. In 1980, Mexico and Central America had 77 million hectares of forested area. In 1990, these areas had 63.5 million hectares of forested area. Find the percent of decrease.

26. The amount won in harness racing in 1991 was $1.238 million. In 1992, the amount was $1.38 million. What was the percent of increase?

27. In 1980, there were about 3 million people in Chicago. In 1990, the population was about 2.8 million people. Find the percent of decrease in the population of Chicago.

28. Caryn was 58 in. tall last year. This year she is 61 in. tall. What is the percent of increase in her height?

29. Last month, Dave weighed 175 lb. This month he weighs 164 lb. What is the percent of decrease in Dave's weight?

Practice 7-7 Markup and Discount

Find the selling price. Round to the nearest cent.

1. cost: $10.00
   markup rate: 60%

2. cost: $12.50
   markup rate: 50%

3. cost: $15.97
   markup rate: 75%

4. cost: $21.00
   markup rate: 100%

5. cost: $25.86
   markup rate: 70%

6. cost: $32.48
   markup rate: 110%

7. cost: $47.99
   markup rate: 160%

8. cost: $87.90
   markup rate: 80%

9. cost: $95.90
   markup rate: 112%

10. cost: $120.00
    markup rate: 56%

11. cost: $150.97
    markup rate: 65%

12. cost: $2,000.00
    markup rate: 95%

Find the sale price. Round to the nearest cent.

13. regular price: $10.00
    discount rate: 10%

14. regular price: $12.00
    discount rate: 15%

15. regular price: $18.95
    discount rate: 20%

16. regular price: $20.95
    discount rate: 15%

17. regular price: $32.47
    discount rate: 20%

18. regular price: $39.99
    discount rate: 25%

19. regular price: $42.58
    discount rate: 30%

20. regular price: $53.95
    discount rate: 35%

21. regular price: $82.99
    discount rate: 50%

22. regular price: $126.77
    discount rate: 62%

23. regular price: $250.98
    discount rate: 70%

24. regular price: $2,000.00
    discount rate: 15%

Find the store's cost. Round to the nearest cent.

25. selling price: $55
    markup rate: 20%

26. selling price: $25.50
    markup rate: 45%

27. selling price: $79.99
    markup rate: 30%

28. selling price: $19.95
    markup rate: 75%

29. selling price: $95
    markup rate: 25%

30. selling price: $64.49
    markup rate: 10%

Practice 7-8 Simple and Compound Interest

Find the final balance for each account. Round your answers to the nearest cent.

1. $800 at 4.25% simple interest for 6 years _____

2. $800 at 6% compounded annually for 4 years _____

3. $250 at 5% simple interest for 3 years _____

4. $900 at 8% simple interest for 1 year _____

5. $1,250 at 5% simple interest for 2 years _____

6. $1,250 at $4\frac{1}{2}$% compounded annually for 3 years _____

7. $1,500 at 4% compounded annually for 4 years _____

8. $1,750 at 5% simple interest for 2 years _____

9. $2,000 at 6% simple interest for 3 years _____

10. $2,000 at 6% compounded annually for 3 years _____

11. $2,500 at 6% compounded annually for 3 years _____

12. $4,000 at 6% compounded annually for 3 years _____

13. $5,000 at 5% simple interest for 10 years _____

14. $6,000 at 5% simple interest for 6 years _____

15. $5,000 at 5% compounded annually for 10 years _____

16. $6,000 at 5% compounded annually for 8 years _____

Solve.

17. Bill invests $500. How much will it grow to in 20 years at 6% compounded annually?

   _____

18. In Exercise 17, how much less will Bill have in the account if the interest is simple interest?

   _____

19. Which earns more compound interest, $1,000 at 5% for 10 years or $1,000 at 10% for 5 years? How much more?

   _____

20. Which earns more simple interest, $1,000 at 5% for 10 years or $1,000 at 10% for 5 years? How much more?

   _____

■■■■ *Practice 7-9* Problem-Solving Strategy: Make a Table

Solve each problem by making a table.

1. Each week, on "Night at the Horse Opera," a couple is asked 10 questions. The couple receives $100 for each question answered correctly. They lose $75 for each incorrect answer. The week that the Andersens played, they won $475. How many questions did they answer correctly? _____

2. How many ways are there to make change for a dollar, using only nickels, dimes, and quarters? _____

3. Luis scored 15 points in a basketball game. How many different combinations of one-, two-, and three-point shots could he have scored? _____

4. You have three $20-bills, two $10-bills, and three $1-bills. How many different dollar amounts could you make with these 8 bills?

   _____

5. In a Ping Pong match, Stephen must win 4 out of 7 games. In how many ways can he do this? _____

6. A target has rings marked 100, 75, 50, and 25 points. You throw four darts and all four hit the target. How many different point totals could you get? _____

7. The sum of two numbers is 32. Their product is 231. What are the two numbers? _____

Use any strategy to solve each problem. If there is not enough information, state what information you need.

8. Tickets for a play cost $6 for adults and $4 for children. One evening, 180 tickets were sold for a total of $960. How many adult tickets were sold for that performance? _____

9. Mr. Jericho's class studied hard for a science exam and raised their class average 15%. How many points did the class average go up?

   _____

   _____

10. Ana is three years older than her husband, Danny. The product of their ages is 3,190. How old is each person? _____

11. Keiko bought 10 CDs. Some cost $12.95 each, the rest cost $15.99 each. She spent $138.62. How many of the $12.95 CDs did she buy? _____

Practice 8-1 Problem-Solving Strategy: Look for a Pattern

Look for a pattern to solve each problem.

1. A series of numbers can be represented by dots arranged in the pattern shown below. If the pattern continues in the same manner, what number is represented by the tenth figure?

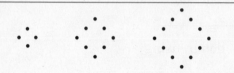

2. Alma sent out 4 cards on Monday, 8 cards on Tuesday, 16 cards on Wednesday, and 28 cards on Thursday. If this pattern continues, how many cards did Alma send out on Saturday?

_____

3. Find the next number in the pattern.
   2, 2, 4, 6, 10, 16, 26, . . . _____

Use any strategy to solve each problem. Show all your work.

4. Jen picked a number, added 9 to it, multiplied the sum by 8, and then subtracted 11. The result was 133. What number did Jen start with? _____

5. Ajani was offered a job in which he was paid $.01 the first day, $.02 the second day, $.04 the third day, $.08 the fourth day, and so on. On which day was Ajani first paid more than $100?

_____

6. Bruno and Grete work in a flower shop. By noon, Bruno had made twice as many flower baskets as Grete. From noon to 3:00 P.M., Grete made 6 more baskets, while Bruno made only 1 more. At 5:00 P.M., Grete had made 10 more flower baskets, while Bruno had made only 3 more. At 5:00 P.M., Bruno had made a total of 4 fewer flower baskets than Grete made all day. How many flower baskets did each make in all?

_____

7. Doug washes his clothes at the laundromat every sixth day. Janelle washes her clothes there every fifteenth day. If they both wash their clothes on the first of May, when will they both wash their clothes on the same day again?

_____

Practice 8-2 Pairs of Angles

Name a pair of vertical angles and a pair of adjacent angles in each figure. Find $m\angle 1$.

1.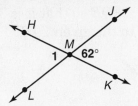

_____

_____

_____

2.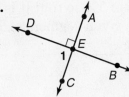

_____

_____

_____

3.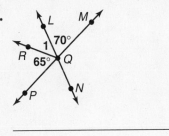

_____

_____

_____

4.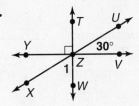

_____

_____

_____

Find the measure of the supplement and the complement of an angle with the given measure.

5. 10°   6. 39°   7. 42.5°   8. $n°$

_____   _____   _____   _____

Use the diagram at the right. Decide whether each statement below is true or false.

9. $\angle GAF$ and $\angle BAC$ are vertical angles. _____

10. $\angle EAF$ and $\angle EAD$ are adjacent angles. _____

11. $\angle CAD$ is a supplement of $\angle DAF$. _____

12. $\angle CAD$ is a complement of $\angle EAF$. _____

13. $m\angle GAC = 90°$ _____

14. $m\angle DAF = 109°$ _____

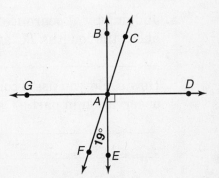

Course 3 Chapter 8

Practice 8-3 *Constructing Segments and Angles*

Use a compass and straightedge to make each construction.

1. Construct segment $\overline{YZ}$ so that it is congruent to the given segment $\overline{AB}$.

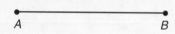

A   B

2. Construct $\angle PQR$ so that it is congruent to the given $\angle DEF$.

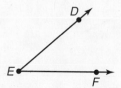

3. Draw an obtuse $\angle G$. Construct an angle congruent to $\angle G$.

4. Use a protractor to draw $\angle XYZ$ with $m\angle XYZ = 36°$. Then use a compass and straightedge to construct $\angle RST$ with the same measure.

5. Construct a segment $\overline{LM}$ so that it is three times the length of the given segment $\overline{JK}$.

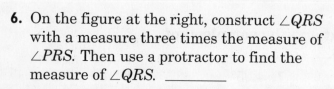

J   K

6. On the figure at the right, construct $\angle QRS$ with a measure three times the measure of $\angle PRS$. Then use a protractor to find the measure of $\angle QRS$. _____

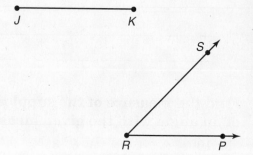

7. Use the figures at the right to complete triangle TUV. First, construct $\overline{TU}$ from the ray given with endpoint U. Make it congruent to $\overline{CD}$. Then draw $\overline{TV}$.

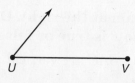

a. Judging by appearance, what might you say about the lengths TU and TV?

_____

b. How could you use a compass to check your observation in part a?

C   D

_____

_____

_____

Practice 8-4 Angles and Parallel Lines

Describe each pair of angles as *vertical, adjacent, corresponding, alternate interior,* or *none of these.*

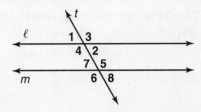

1. ∠7, ∠5

_____

2. ∠1, ∠2

_____

3. ∠1, ∠5

_____

4. ∠1, ∠7

_____

5. ∠4, ∠7

_____

6. ∠4, ∠5

_____

Use the figure at the right for Exercises 7 and 8.

7. Name four pairs of corresponding angles.

_____

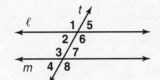

8. Name two pairs of alternate interior angles.

_____

In each diagram below, line ℓ is parallel to line m. Find the measures of the numbered angles in each diagram.

9.

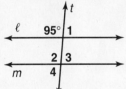

m∠1 = _____

m∠2 = _____

m∠3 = _____

m∠4 = _____

10.

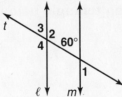

m∠1 = _____

m∠2 = _____

m∠3 = _____

m∠4 = _____

11.

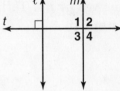

m∠1 = _____

m∠2 = _____

m∠3 = _____

m∠4 = _____

12. Use the figure at the right. Judging by appearance, is line ℓ parallel to line m? Explain how you could use a protractor to support your conjecture.

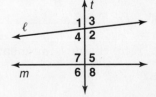

_____

_____

_____

_____

Practice 8-5 *Exploring Congruent Triangles*

Are the triangles congruent? If so, write the congruence and tell why they are congruent.

1.

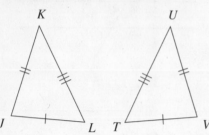

2.

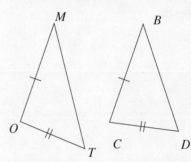

_____

_____

3.

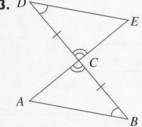

4.

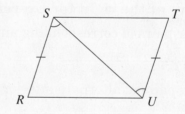

_____

_____

Answer *yes* or *no*. Tell whether each triangle below must be congruent to △*XYZ* at the right.

5.

6.

7.

_____   _____   _____

Use the triangles at the right to answer the following.

8. △*DEF* ≅ _____ by _____

9. Find the missing measures for △*DEF*.

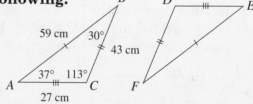

_____

Practice 8-6 Quadrilaterals and Triangles

Judging by appearance, classify each quadrilateral. Name the congruent sides and angles.

1.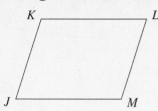

2.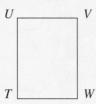

3.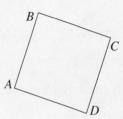

_____

_____

_____

Label each quadrilateral as a _square, rectangle, parallelogram,_ or _rhombus._ Choose the best name for the figure.

4.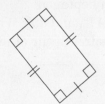

5.

6.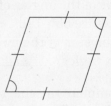

_____

_____

_____

7.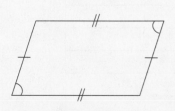

8.

9. △ABC ≅ △CDA

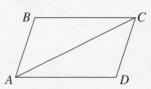

_____

_____

Which labels apply: _acute, right, obtuse, scalene, isosceles,_ or _equilateral?_

10.

11.

12.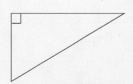

_____

_____

_____

Practice 8-7 Angles of Polygons

Classify each polygon by the number of its sides.

1.  _____

2. _____

3. _____

4.  _____

5. a polygon with 8 sides

_____

6. a polygon with 10 sides

_____

7. Find the measure of each angle of a regular hexagon.

_____

8. The measures of four angles of a pentagon are 143°, 118°, 56°, and 97°. Find the measure of the fifth angle. _____

9. What is the sum of the measures of the angles in a figure having 9 sides?

_____

10. What is the sum of the measures of the angles of a figure having 11 sides?

_____

11. Four of the angles of a hexagon measure 53°, 126°, 89°, and 117°. What is the sum of the measures of the other two angles? _____

12. Four of the angles of a heptagon measure 109°, 158°, 117°, and 89°. What is the sum of the measures of the other three angles? _____

13. Complete the chart for the number of diagonals in each polygon. The first three have been done for you.

Polygon	Number of Sides	Number of Diagonals
triangle	3	0
rectangle	4	2
pentagon	5	5
hexagon		
heptagon		
octagon		
nonagon		
decagon		

14. From the table you completed in Exercise 13, what pattern do you see? Explain.

_____

_____

Practice 8-8 Polygons and Tessellations

Trace or cut out each figure. Show how each can be used in a tessellation.

1.
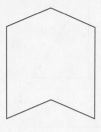

2.
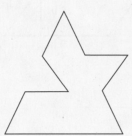

3.
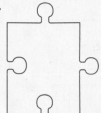

4.
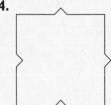

5.

6.

Start with the basic shape shown. Modify it to make a design. Trace or cut out your design or use graph paper to make a tessellation.

7.

8.

9.
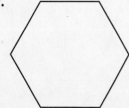

10.

Course 3 Chapter 8

Practice 8-9 Areas of Parallelograms and Triangles

Find the area of each parallelogram.

1.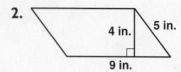

9 cm   10 cm
20 cm

_____

2.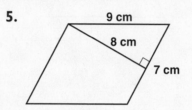

4 in.   5 in.
9 in.

_____

3.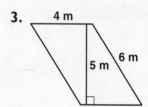

4 m
5 m   6 m

_____

4.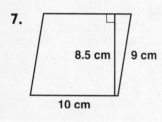

6.2 yd
3.5 yd

_____

5.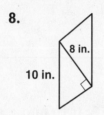

9 cm
8 cm
7 cm

_____

6.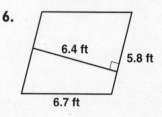

6.4 ft   5.8 ft
6.7 ft

_____

7.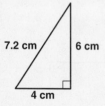

8.5 cm   9 cm
10 cm

_____

8.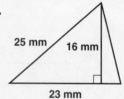

8 in.
10 in.

_____

9.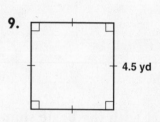

4.5 yd

_____

10. The area of a parallelogram is 221 yd². Its height is 13 yd. What is the length of its corresponding base?

_____

11. The area of a parallelogram is 116 cm². Its base is 8 cm. What is the corresponding height?

_____

Choose a calculator, paper and pencil, or mental math to find the area of each triangle.

12.

7.2 cm   6 cm
4 cm

_____

13.

25 mm   16 mm
23 mm

_____

14.

22 in.
19 in.   18 in.

_____

Name _____ Class _____ Date _____

Practice 8-10 Areas and Circumferences of Circles

Use a calculator to find the circumference and area of each
circle. Round your answers to the nearest hundredth.

1.
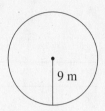

2.
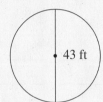

3.

_____   _____   _____

4.
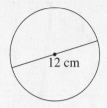

5.
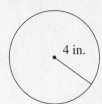

6.
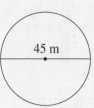

_____   _____   _____

_____   _____   _____

Find the circumference of a circle with the given diameter

or radius. Use $\frac{22}{7}$ for π.

7. $d = 70$ cm   **8.** $r = 14$ cm   **9.** $d = 35$ in.

_____   _____   _____

Find the radius and the diameter of a circle with the given
circumference. Round your answers to the nearest
hundredth.

10. $C = 68$ cm   **11.** $C = 150$ m   **12.** $C = 218$ in.

_____   _____   _____

_____   _____   _____

13. Use the figure at the right. Find the area of the
shaded region. Round your answer to the nearest
hundredth.

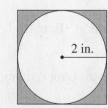

_____

Practice 9-1 Three-Dimensional Figures

For each figure, describe the base of the figure and name the figure.

1.

2.

3.

4.

_____

_____

5.

6.

7.

8.

_____

_____

Name each three-dimensional figure.

9. bowling ball   10. VCR   11. soup can   12. funnel

_____

Complete.

13. A _____ has exactly two circular bases.

14. A hexagonal prism has ___ faces.

15. A cube has ___ edges.

16. A pentagonal pyramid has ___ faces.

17. A pentagonal pyramid has ___ edges.

18. A rectangular prism has ___ vertices.

Circle A, B, C, or D. Match each description with the correct name.

19. A space figure with six congruent square faces.

   A. triangular prism   **B.** cylinder   **C.** cube   **D.** pyramid

20. A space figure with parallel bases that are congruent, parallel circles.

   A. rectangular prism **B.** cylinder   **C.** cube   **D.** all three

Draw.

21. On a sheet of graph paper, draw a rectangular prism.

Practice 9-2 *Drawing Three-Dimensional Figures*

Draw the base plan for the stacked cubes.

1.

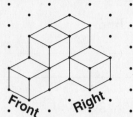

2.

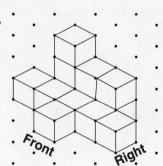

Draw the top, front, and right views of each figure.

3.

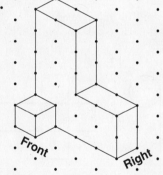

4.

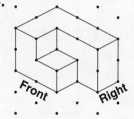

Practice 9-3 Unfolding Three-Dimensional Figures

List the shapes and the number of each that are found in a net for the given figure.

1. rectangular prism

_____

_____

2. pentagonal pyramid

_____

_____

3. cylinder

_____

_____

4. triangular pyramid

_____

_____

5. cone

_____

_____

6. hexagonal prism

_____

_____

7. Draw a net for a rectangular box that is 9 cm long, 5 cm wide, and 3 cm tall.

8. Draw a net for a cylinder whose height is 8 in. and whose radius is 3 in.

Name the space figure for each net.

9.

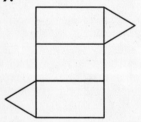

_____

_____

10.

_____

_____

11.

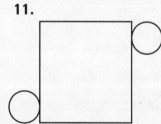

_____

_____

12.

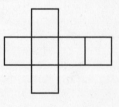

_____

_____

13. Circle A, B, C, or D. Which three-dimensional figure can be made from this net?

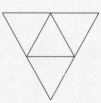

   A. triangular prism   **B.** rectangular prism

   C. cube   **D.** triangular pyramid

Practice 9-4 Precision and Significant Digits

Choose the more precise unit of measure.

1. week, day _____   2. gallon, cup _____   3. ounce, ton _____

4. mile, yard _____   5. day, hour _____   6. quart, pint _____

Choose the more precise measurement.

7. 1.9 in., 7 in.   8. 6 ft, $1\frac{1}{3}$ ft   9. $\frac{1}{8}$ mi, $\frac{2}{3}$ mi

_____   _____   _____

10. 13 h, 5 min   11. $\frac{1}{2}$ c, $\frac{1}{2}$ qt   12. $91, $2.43

_____   _____   _____

Compute. Round your answer to match the least precise measurement.

13. 31.7 m − 18 m   14. 7.34 mi + 19.9 mi   15. $2\frac{3}{8}$ in. + $6\frac{1}{2}$ in.

_____   _____   _____

16. 12.745 cm − 3.25 cm   17. $8\frac{5}{6}$ in. − $3\frac{3}{4}$ in.   18. 14.8 km + 13.57 km

_____   _____   _____

How many significant digits are in each number?

19. 12,954 _____   20. 180 _____   21. 30,220 _____

22. 6.905 _____   23. 0.901 _____   24. 0.044 _____

25. 15.093 _____   26. 0.701 _____   27. 9.006 _____

28. 15.0901 _____   29. 451.09040 _____   30. 60.06 _____

Compute. Use significant digits.

31. 13.4 × 2.7 _____   32. 28.74 ÷ 5.6 _____   33. 133 ÷ 14.71 _____

34. 56.06 ÷ 8.1 _____   35. 19.8 × 0.02 _____   36. 3,000 ÷ 56 _____

37. Use significant digits to compute the area of a rectangle with
    length 2.9 m and width 1.80 m. _____

38. Use significant digits to compute the area of a square whose
    side measures 9.32 cm. _____

39. Use significant digits to compute the area of a rectangular
    swimming pool with length 23.02 m and width 16 m. _____

Practice 9-5 *Surface Areas of Prisms and Cylinders*

Find the surface area of each figure to the nearest square unit.

1.
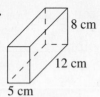
8 cm
12 cm
5 cm

_____

2.

8 m   15 m
6 m

_____

3.
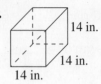
14 in.
14 in.
14 in.

_____

4.
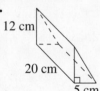
12 cm
20 cm
5 cm

_____

5.
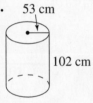
7 ft   75 ft
8 ft

_____

6.
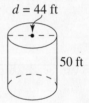
8 m   23m
15 m

_____

7.
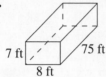
53 cm
102 cm

_____

8.
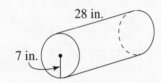
28 in.
7 in.

_____

9.
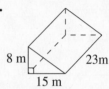
$d = 44$ ft
50 ft

_____

Rachel and Sam are going to paint the exposed surfaces of each figure. Find the area to be painted to the nearest square unit.

10.
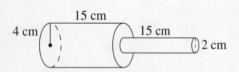
15 cm
4 cm   15 cm
2 cm

_____

11.
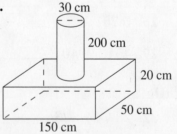
30 cm
200 cm
20 cm
50 cm
150 cm

_____

12.

4 ft
2 ft

This cylinder does not have a top.

_____

Practice 9-6 *Surface Areas of Pyramids and Cones*

Find the surface area of each square pyramid to the nearest square unit.

1.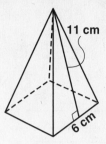
11 cm
6 cm

_____

2.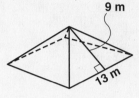
9 m
13 m

_____

3.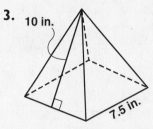
10 in.
7.5 in.

_____

4.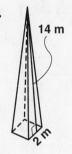
14 m
2 m

_____

5.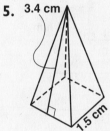
3.4 cm
1.5 cm

_____

6.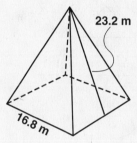
23.2 m
16.8 m

_____

Find the surface area of each cone to the nearest square unit. Use $\pi = 3.14$.

7.
14 ft
8 ft

_____

8. 10.6 ft
4.2 ft

_____

9.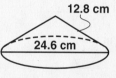
12.8 cm
24.6 cm

_____

10.
23.4 m
18.02 m

_____

11.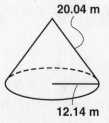
20.04 m
12.14 m

_____

12.
17.3 in.
6.90 in.

_____

Course 3 Chapter 9

Practice 9-7 Volumes of Prisms and Cylinders

Find the volume of each figure to the nearest cubic unit.

1.
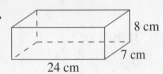
8 cm
7 cm
24 cm

_____

2.
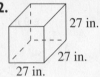
27 in.
27 in.
27 in.

_____

3.
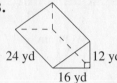
24 yd
12 yd
16 yd

_____

4.
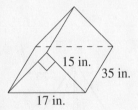
15 in.
35 in.
17 in.

_____

5.
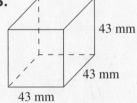
43 mm
43 mm
43 mm

_____

6.
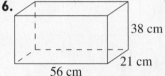
38 cm
21 cm
56 cm

_____

7.   5 cm
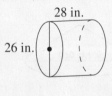
12 cm

_____

8.   48 mm
14 mm
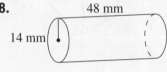

_____

9.   16 in.

27 in.

_____

10.   28 in.
26 in.
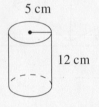

_____

11.   2 ft
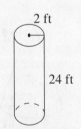
24 ft

_____

12.
42 ft
7 ft
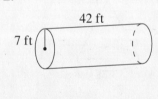

_____

13. Suppose you want to buy concrete for a patio 36 ft by 24 ft by 9 in. If concrete costs $55/yd^3, how much will the concrete for the patio cost?

_____

14. A cylinder has a volume of about 500 cm^3 and a height of 10 cm. What is the length of the radius to the nearest tenth of a cm?

_____

Practice 9-8 Proportions and Changing Dimensions

Complete the table for each prism.

	Original Size		Doubled Dimensions		
	Dimensions (m)	S.A. (m²)	Dimensions (m)	S.A. (m²)	New S.A. ÷ Old S.A.
1.	$2 \times 3 \times 4$				
2.	$5 \times 5 \times 9$				
3.	$7 \times 7 \times 7$				
4.	$8 \times 12 \times 15$				
5.	$15 \times 15 \times 20$				
6.	$32 \times 32 \times 32$				

7. What conclusion can you draw?

_____

_____

8. A rectangular prism is 8 cm by 10 cm by 15 cm. What are the volume and surface area of the prism?

_____

9. In Exercise 8, if each dimension of the prism is tripled, what are the new volume and surface area?

_____

Use the triangular prism shown at the right for Exercises 10 and 11.

10. Find the volume and surface area.

_____

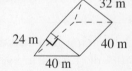

11. If each dimension of the prism is doubled, what are the new volume and surface areas?

_____

12. A rectangular prism is 9 in. long, 15 in. wide, and 21 in. high. The length is doubled. What happens to the volume?

_____

13. A rectangular prism is 8 cm long, 24 cm wide, and 43 cm high. The length is doubled, and the width is tripled. What happens to the volume?

_____

Practice 9-9 Problem-Solving Strategy: Use Multiple Strategies

Solve using any strategies. Show all your work.

1. You can cut square corners off an 8 in. by 10 in. piece of cardboard to get a pattern that you could fold into a box without a top.

   a. What dimensions for the corners, to the nearest half-inch, will give the greatest volume? _____

   b. What is the greatest volume of the box? _____

2. Corinda has 400 ft of fencing to make a play area. She wants the fenced area to be rectangular. What dimensions should she use in order to enclose the maximum possible area?

   _____

3. A restaurant dining room measures 100 ft by 150 ft. The height of the room is 9 ft. If the occupancy guidelines recommend at least 150 ft^3 per person, what is the maximum number of people that can be in the room? _____

4. Maurice lives at point A. The library is at point B. How many different routes can Maurice take from home to the library if he only goes to the right and down, never retracing his route? _____

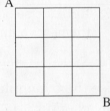

5. The consecutive even integers from 2 to n are 2, 4, 6, . . . , n. The square of the sum of the integers is 5,184. What is the value of n?

   _____

6. A bicyclist has 120 mi to cover on a trip. One day she bicycles 40% of the distance. The next day she cycles 60% of the remaining distance. How much further does she have to cycle?

   _____

Use the dartboard shown at the right.

7. Three darts are thrown at the target. If each dart lands on the target, how many different point totals are possible?

   _____

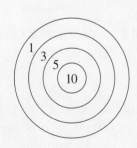

8. If 4 darts are thrown at the target and each dart lands on the target, how many point totals are possible ?

   _____

Practice 9-10 Volumes of Pyramids and Cones

Find the volume of each cone or pyramid to the nearest cubic unit.

1.

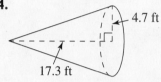

9 cm
6 cm
6 cm

_____

2.

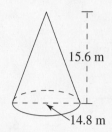

15.6 m

14.8 m

_____

3.

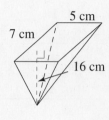

5 cm
7 cm
16 cm

_____

4.

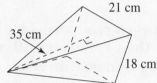

4.7 ft
17.3 ft

_____

5.

21 cm
35 cm
18 cm

_____

6.

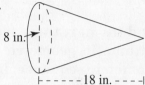

8 in.
18 in.

_____

Find the missing dimension for each three-dimensional figure to the nearest tenth, given the volume and other dimensions.

7. rectangular pyramid,
   $l = 8$ m, $w = 4.6$ m, $V = 88$ m³

   _____

8. cone, $r = 5$ in., $V = 487$ in.³

   _____

9. square pyramid, $s = 14$ yd, $V = 489$ yd³

   _____

10. square pyramid, $h = 8.9$ cm, $V = 56$ cm³

    _____

11. cone, $h = 18$ cm, $V = 986$ cm³

    _____

12. cone, $r = 5.5$ ft, $V = 592$ ft³

    _____

13. Find the volume of a rectangular prism 4 ft by 2 ft by 3 ft with a cylindrical hole, radius 6 in., through the center.

    _____

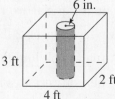

6 in.
3 ft
4 ft
2 ft

14. Margarite has a cylindrical tin of popcorn that is 18 in. tall and has a radius of 4 in. She wants to use the tin for something else and needs to empty the popcorn into a box. The box is 8 in. long, 8 in. wide, and 14 in. tall. Will the popcorn fit in the box? Explain.

    _____

    _____

■■■■Practice 10-1 Patterns and Sequences

Write a rule to describe each sequence. Then find the next three terms in the sequence.

1. 3, 8, 13, 18, ___, ___, ___

_____

2. 7, 14, 28, 56, ___ , ___ , ___

_____

3. 32, 8, 2, $\frac{1}{2}$, ___, ___, ___

_____

4. 14, 11, 8, 5, ___ , ___ , ___

_____

5. 35, 23, 11, −1, _____, _____, _____

_____

6. 3,000, 300, 30, 3, _____ , _____ , _____

_____

Find the next three terms in each sequence. Identify each as arithmetic, geometric, or neither. For each arithmetic or geometric sequence, find the common difference or ratio.

7. 7.1, 7.5, 7.9, 8.3, ___ , ___ , ___

_____

8. 5, 6, 8, 11, 15, 20, ___ , ___ , ___

_____

9. 8,000, 4,000, 2,000, 1,000, ___ , ___ , ___

_____

10. 92, 89, 86, 83, ___ , ___ , ___

_____

11. −1, 2, −4, 8, ___ , ___ , ___

_____

12. 2.3, 2.03, 2.003, 2.0003, ___ , ___ , ___

_____

13. 1, 3, 6, 8, 16, 18, 36, ___ , ___ , ___

_____

14. 140, 133, 126, 119, ___ , ___ , ___

_____

15. 3, 9, 27, 81, ___ , ___ , ___

_____

16. 540, 270, 90, 22.5, ___ , ___ , ___

_____

Tell whether each situation produces an *arithmetic sequence*, a *geometric sequence*, or *neither*.

17. The temperature rises at the rate of 0.75°F per hour. _____

18. A person loses 2 lb each month. _____

19. A toadstool doubles in size each week. _____

20. A person receives a 6% raise each year. _____

Solve.

21. On the planet Syzer, any plant grows 3 in. one day and shrinks $2\frac{1}{3}$ in. the next. Mary measured a plant and found it just over 18 in. tall. What is the greatest age (in days) possible for Mary's plant? _____

Practice 10-2 Functions

Complete the table of input/output pairs for each function.

1. $y = 3x$

Input x	Output y
4	
8	
12	
16	

2. $z = 15n$

Input n	Output z
1	
2	
3	
	60

3. $d = 30 - s$

Input s	Output d
0	
5	
	20
	15

4. $h = 120 \div g$

Input g	Output h
2	
6	
	10
15	

5. $r = 2t - 1$

Input t	Output r
3	
9	
20	
	99

6. $p = 2v - 12$

Input v	Output p
	6
	40
43	
75	

Does each situation represent a function? Explain.

7. Input: the distance that needs to be biked

Output: the time it takes if you bike at 5 mi/h

_____

8. Input: the time of day you go to the grocery store

Output: the cost of the groceries

_____

9. Input: the number of copies of a book

Output: the total cost of the books

_____

10. Input: a T-shirt color

Output: the T-shirt cost

_____

Use the function $f(x) = 5x + 1$. Find each output.

11. $f(3)$ _____   **12.** $f(-6)$ _____   **13.** $f(8)$ _____   **14.** $f(-2)$ _____

15. $f(1.5)$ _____   **16.** $f(25)$ _____   **17.** $f(30)$ _____   **18.** $f(100)$ _____

Use the function rule $f(n) = 4n^2 - 1$. Find each output.

19. $f(0)$ _____   **20.** $f(1)$ _____   **21.** $f(-1)$ _____   **22.** $f(2)$ _____

23. $f(-2)$ _____   **24.** $f(3)$ _____   **25.** $f(2.5)$ _____   **26.** $f(5)$ _____

Practice 10-3 Graphing Linear Functions

Make a table of input/output pairs for each function. Then graph the function. Show only the part that makes sense for each situation.

1. On a trip Alex averages 300 mi/d. The distance he covers (output) is a function of the number of days (input).

Input				
Output				

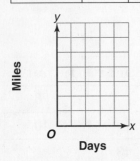

2. Suppose you earn $7 per hour. The number of hours you work (input) determines your pay (output).

Input				
Output				

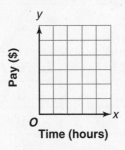

3. Suppose you have $50. The amount of money you spend (input) decreases the amount you have left (output).

Input				
Output				

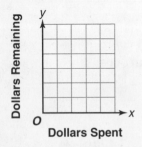

4. You have $10.00. Each week you save $2.50. The number of weeks you save (input) increases your savings (output).

Input				
Output				

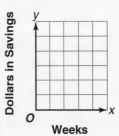

Use the axes provided to graph each linear function.

5. $f(x) = -x + 4$

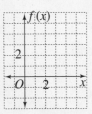

6. $f(x) = \frac{2}{3}x + 1$

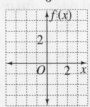

7. $f(x) = -2x + 1$

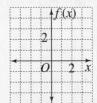

Practice 10-4 Writing Rules for Linear Functions

Write a linear function rule for each situation. Identify the input and output variables.

1. Amy sells tote bags at a craft fair for a day. She pays $50 to rent a booth. The materials and labor cost on each tote bag is $3.50. Her expenses for the day depend on how many tote bags she sells.

   _____

2. Ms. Watson receives a base pay of $150, plus a commission of $45 on each appliance that she sells. Her total pay depends on how many appliances she sells.

   _____

For each graph, find the slope and *y*-intercept. Use the values to write the function rule for each graph.

3.

4.

5.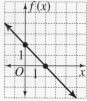

_____   _____   _____

6.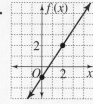

7.

8.

_____   _____   _____

Do the data in each table represent a linear function? If so, write the function rule.

9.

Input	0	1	2	3	4
Output	2	5	8	11	14

_____

10.

Input	0	1	2	3	4
Output	0	2	5	2	0

_____

11.

Input	-2	0	4	6	8
Output	-1	-3	-7	-9	-11

_____

12.

Input	-3	-2	-1	0	1
Output	-1	1	2	2	2

_____

Practice 10-5 Problem-Solving Strategy: Solve a Simpler Problem

Use the strategy of solving a simpler problem.
Look at the figure at the right.

1. What is the number of dots in the portion of the figure
   labeled 1? _____

2. The portion is extended to include that labeled 2. Now
   what is the total number of dots?
   _____

3. Find the total number of dots when the figure is extended to
   include 3; to include 4.
   _____

4. Suppose you extend the figure to include a portion 10. How
   many dots would there be in the figure?
   _____

5. Is the total number of dots a function of the number of portions?
   If so, write the rule in function notation.
   _____

Use any strategy to solve the problem.

6. Myrna checked out a book from the library that has 558 pages.
   How many times will she see the number 5 in the page
   numbers?
   _____

7. The sum of two integers is −18. Their difference is 12. What are
   the two integers? _____

8. Paper cups come in packages of 24 or 30. Phyllis bought 12
   packages and a total of 318 paper cups. How many of each size
   package did she buy?
   _____

9. Jerome delivers newspapers. He earns $5 a week, plus $.20 for
   each paper he delivers. How many papers must he deliver to
   earn $25 a week? _____

Practice 10-6 Relating Graphs to Events

Each graph represents a situation. Match a graph with the appropriate situation. Explain your choices.

a.
Time

b.
Time

c.
Time

d.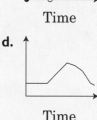
Time

e.
Time

f.
Time

1. the amount of an unpaid library fine _____

2. the height above ground of a skydiver during a dive _____

3. one's adrenaline flow when receiving a fright _____

4. the temperature of the air during a 24-h period beginning at 9:00 A.M. _____.

5. oven temperature for baking cookies _____

6. elevator ride up with stops _____

7. Draw a graph that will show the height of a football after it has been kicked.

8. Draw the graph of the distance traveled by a car that was driving 50 mi/h, but is now stopped by road construction.

Circle A, B, or C. Which graph best describes the information?

9. The function table at the right describes the distance in feet that an object falls over time.

Time (s)	Distance (ft)
1	16
2	64
3	144
4	256

A.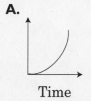
Time

B.
Time

C.
Time

▰▰▰ *Practice 10-7* Quadratic Functions

Write a rule for each quadratic function.

1.

x	0	1	2	3	4
$f(x)$	3	4	7	12	19

_____

2.

x	−2	−1	0	1	2
$f(x)$	−8	−2	0	−2	−8

_____

3.

x	−1	0	1	2	3
$f(x)$	4	0	4	16	36

_____

4.

x	−10	−5	0	5	10
$f(x)$	95	20	−5	20	95

_____

Tell whether (1, 3) lies on the graph of each function.

5. $f(x) = x^2 + 1$ **6.** $f(x) = x^2 + 2$ **7.** $f(x) = 2x^2 - 1$ **8.** $f(x) = 2x^2 - x + 2$

_____   _____   _____   _____

For each quadratic function, complete the table and then sketch the graph.

9. $f(x) = x^2 + 1$

x	$x^2 + 1 = f(x)$
−3	
−2	
−1	
0	
1	
2	
3	

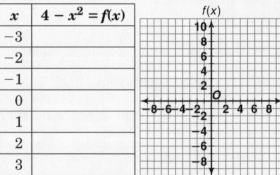

10. $f(x) = 4 - x^2$

x	$4 - x^2 = f(x)$
−3	
−2	
−1	
0	
1	
2	
3	

Make a table of values for each function. Use integers from −3 to 3 for inputs. Then graph the function.

11. $f(x) = x^2 - 2$

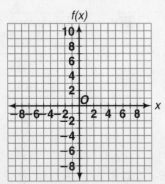

12. $f(x) = -x^2 + 2x$

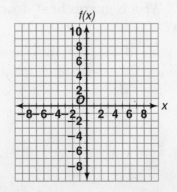

Practice 10-8 Other Nonlinear Functions

Complete the table. Plot the points. Then draw a curve through the points to graph the function.

1. $f(x) = \frac{20}{x}$

x	f(x)
2	
4	
5	
10	

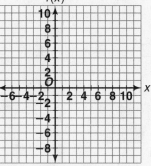

2. $f(x) = \frac{12}{x} + 2$

x	f(x)
2	
3	
4	
6	

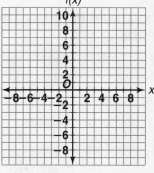

3. $f(x) = 2^x - 1$

x	f(x)
-1	
0	
1	
2	
3	

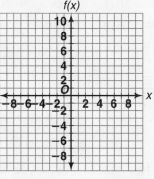

4. $f(x) = 32\left(\frac{1}{2}\right)^x$

x	f(x)
2	
3	
4	
5	
6	

Does the point (2, 2) lie on the graph of each function?

5. $f(x) = 2x - 2$

_____

6. $f(x) = \left(\frac{1}{2}\right)^x$

_____

7. $f(x) = x^2 - x$

_____

8. $f(x) = \frac{4}{x}$

_____

Does the point (1, 6) lie on the graph of each function?

9. $f(x) = 3x + 2$

_____

10. $f(x) = x^2 + 5$

_____

11. $f(x) = 6^x$

_____

12. $f(x) = \frac{10}{x}$

_____

13. Suppose you put $25 into an account that pays 10% interest compounded annually. The function $f(x) = 25(1.10)^x$ describes the amount of money in the account after x years.

a. Find $f(2)$. _____

b. Graph the function for input values 0 to 6.

c. Estimate when the balance will first exceed $50.

_____

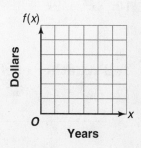

 *Practice 10-9* Exploring Polynomials

In Exercises 1–5

 represents x^2, ▯ represents x, ▢ represents 1,

 represents $-x^2$, ▮ represents $-x$, ▪ represents -1.

Write a variable expression for each model.

1.

_____

2.

_____

3.

_____

Write and simplify the polynomials represented by each model.

4.

_____

5.

_____

Choose tiles or properties to simplify each polynomial.

6. $2x^2 - x^2 + 7x - 2x + 5$

_____

7. $3x^2 + 2x - 8x + 6$

_____

8. $x^2 - 4x^2 + x + 5x - 8 + 3$

_____

9. $x^2 + 6x + x^2 - 4x + 1 - 5$

_____

10. $3x^2 + 2x + 3x + 3 - 1$

_____

11. $x^2 + 3x^2 + 3x - 9 + 2x$

_____

Tell whether each function is *linear* or *quadratic*.

12. $f(x) = x^2 - 5$

_____

13. $f(x) = 3x + 2$

_____

14. $f(x) = 10$

_____

Practice 10-10 *Adding and Subtracting Polynomials*

In Exercises 1–5

▢ represents x^2,   ▯ represents x,   ▢ represents 1,

◼ represents $-x^2$,   ▮ represents $-x$,   ◼ represents -1.

Write the addition problem modeled in each exercise.
Then find the sum.

1.   2.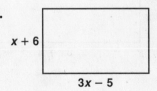

_____   _____

Add.

3. $5x - 4$
   $6x + 2$

_____

4. $3x^2 - 6x$
   $x^2 + 2x$

_____

5. $7x^2 + 3x - 5$
   $-4x^2 - x + 4$

_____

6. $(x^2 - 2x) + (4x^2 + 7)$

_____

7. $(2x^2 + 8) + (3x^2 - 9)$

_____

8. $(7x^2 + 3x - 5) + (x^2 - 6x + 4)$

_____

9. $(5x^2 - 3x + 3) + (4x - 5)$

_____

Find the perimeter of each figure.

10.
x ▢
$x + 5$

_____

11.
$2x$ \ $2x + 5$
$3x$

_____

12.
$x + 6$ ▢
$3x - 5$

_____

Choose tiles or use coefficients to subtract.

13. $(4x^2 + 1) - (x^2 + 3)$

_____

14. $(2x^2 + 2x) - (8x + 7)$

_____

15. $(3x^2 + 7x - 5) - (x^2 - 4x - 1)$

_____

16. $(x^2 - 2x + 7) - (3x^2 - 9x + 2)$

_____

17. $(6x^2 + 8x + 1) - (4x^2 - 8x + 7)$

_____

18. $(4x^2 - 6x + 3) - (2x^2 - 7x - 9)$

_____

Practice 10-11 Multiplying Polynomials

Find the area of each rectangle.

1.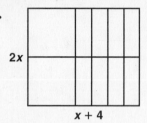

2.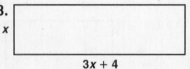

3.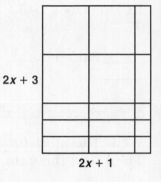

_____   _____   _____

Multiply.

4. $x^2 \cdot x^2$

5. $7x \cdot 2x$

6. $(-3x)x$

7. $(4x^2)(-2x)$

_____   _____   _____   _____

8. $5x^2 \cdot 2x^2$

9. $(-x)(7x^2)$

10. $(3x^2)(-2x^3)$

11. $(-x)(-8x^2)$

_____   _____   _____   _____

Use the distributive property to find each product.

12. $x(x + 2)$

13. $3x(x - 5)$

14. $2x^2(x + 9)$

_____   _____   _____

15. $2(x^2 + 8x + 1)$

16. $2x^2(4x + 1)$

17. $3x(x^2 + 4x - 6)$

_____   _____   _____

Find the area of each figure.

18.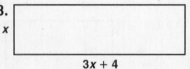

19.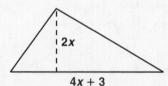

20.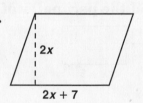

_____   _____   _____

Circle A, B, C, or D.

21. Multiply $4x$ by $-x^2 + 2x - 9$.

    A. $4x^2 + 8x + 36$ **B.** $-8x^3 + 4x^2 + 36x$

    C. $-4x^3 + 8x^2 - 36x$ **D.** $-x^3 + 8x^2 - 36x$

22. Multiply $-6x$ by $-2x^2 - 3x + 1$.

    A. $12x^3 - 18x^2 + 6x$ **B.** $12x^3 - 18x^2 - 6x$

    C. $-12x^3 + 18x^2 + 6x$ **D.** $12x^3 + 18x^2 - 6x$

Practice 11-1 *Counting Outcomes*

Draw a tree diagram to show all possibilities.

1. Today, the school's cafeteria is offering a choice of pizza or spaghetti. You can get milk or juice to drink. For dessert you can get pudding or an apple. You must take one of each choice.

2. A clothing store sells shirts in three sizes: small, medium, and large. The shirts come with buttons or with snaps. The colors available are blue or beige.

Choose a calculator, paper and pencil, or mental math.

3. How many license plates are possible if four letters are to be followed by two digits?

   _____

4. How many license plates are possible if two letters are to be followed by four digits?

   _____

5. A dress pattern offers two styles of skirts, three styles of sleeves, and four different collars. How many different types of dresses are available from one pattern?

   _____

6. In a class of 250 eighth graders, 14 are running for president, 12 are running for vice president, 9 are running for secretary, and 13 are running for treasurer. How many different results are possible for the class election?

   _____

7. A home alarm system has a 3-digit code that can be used to deactivate the system. If the homeowner forgets the code, how many different codes might the homeowner have to try?

   _____

8. A 4-letter password is required to enter a computer file. How many passwords are possible if no letter is repeated and nonsense words are allowed?

   _____

■■■■■Practice 11-2 Permutations

Use a calculator, paper and pencil, or mental math to evaluate each factorial.

1. 6!

2. 12!

3. 9!

4. $\frac{8!}{5!}$

5. $\frac{12!}{3!}$

_____

6. $_9P_5$

7. $_8P_2$

8. $_{10}P_8$

9. $_5P_5$

10. $_{15}P_6$

_____

Solve.

11. In how many ways can all the letters of the word WORK be arranged?

_____

12. In how many ways can you arrange seven friends in a row for a photo?

_____

13. A disk jockey can play eight songs in one time slot. In how many different orders can the eight songs be played?

_____

14. Melody has nine bowling trophies to arrange in a horizontal line on a shelf. How many arrangements are possible?

15. At a track meet, 42 students entered the 100-m race. In how many ways can first, second, and third places be awarded?

_____

16. In how many ways can a president, a vice president, and a treasurer be chosen from a group of 15 people running for office?

_____

17. A car dealer has 38 used cars to sell. Each day two cars are chosen for advertising specials. One car appears in a television commercial and the other appears in a newspaper advertisement. In how many ways can the two cars be chosen?

_____

18. A bicycle rack outside a classroom has room for six bicycles. In the class, 10 students sometimes ride their bicycles to school. How many different arrangements of bicycles are possible for any given day?

_____

19. A certain type of luggage has room for three initials. How many different 3-letter arrangements of letters are possible?

_____

20. A roller coaster has room for 10 people. The people sit single file, one after the other. How many different arrangements are possible for 10 passengers on the roller coaster?

_____

Name _____ Class _____ Date _____

Practice 11-3 Combinations

Compute each number of combinations.

1. $_9C_1$ _____   2. $_8C_4$ _____   3. $_{11}C_4$ _____   4. $_{11}C_7$ _____

5. $_4C_4$ _____   6. $_9C_3$ _____   7. $_{12}C_6$ _____   8. $_8C_2$ _____

9. 3 videos from 10 _____   10. 2 letters from LOVE _____   11. 4 books from 8 _____   12. 5 people from 7 _____

Solve.

13. Ten students from a class have volunteered to be on a committee to organize a dance. In how many ways can six be chosen for the committee?

_____

14. Twenty-three people try out for extra parts in a play. In how many ways can eight people be chosen to be extras?

_____

15. A team of nine players is to be chosen from 15 available players. In how many ways can this be done?

_____

16. In a talent show, five semi-finalists are chosen from 46 entries. In how many ways can the semi-finalists be chosen?

_____

17. At a party there are 12 people present. The host requests that each person present shake hands exactly once with every other person. How many handshakes are necessary?

_____

18. In math class there are 24 students. The teacher picks 4 students to serve on the bulletin board committee. How many different committees of 4 are possible?

_____

19. Five friends, Billi, Joe, Eduardo, Mari, and Xavier, want one photograph taken of each possible pair of friends. Use B, J, E, M, and X, and list all of the pairs that need to be photographed.

_____

_____

20. **Circle A, B, C, or D.**

Which situation described has $_8C_3$ possible outcomes?

A. Select three letters from 8 to form a 3-letter password.

B. Find the possible ways that first, second, and third prize winners can be selected from 8 contestants.

C. Arrange 8 people in 3 rows.

D. Pick a team of 3 people from 8 players.

Practice 11-4 *Theoretical and Experimental Probability*

A dart is thrown at the game board shown. Find each probability.

1. $P(A)$ _____   **2.** $P(B)$ _____   **3.** $P(C)$ _____

4. $P(\text{not } A)$ _____   **5.** $P(\text{not } B)$ _____   **6.** $P(\text{not } C)$ _____

The odds in favor of winning a game are 5 to 9.

7. Find the probability of winning the game. _____

8. Find the probability of *not* winning the game. _____

A bag of uninflated balloons contains 10 red, 12 blue, 15 yellow, and 8 green balloons. A balloon is drawn at random. Find each probability.

9. $P(\text{red})$ _____   **10.** $P(\text{blue})$ _____   **11.** $P(\text{yellow})$ _____   **12.** $P(\text{green})$ _____

13. What are the odds in favor of picking a blue balloon? _____

14. What are the odds in favor of picking a green balloon? _____

15. What is the probability of picking a balloon that is not yellow? _____

16. What is the probability of picking a balloon that is not red? _____

Solve.

17. a. You are given a ticket for the weekly drawing at the grocery store each time you enter the store. Last week you were in the store once. There are 1,200 tickets in the box. Find the probability and the odds of your winning.

_____

b. Find the probability and odds of your winning if you were in the store three times last week and there are 1,200 tickets in the box. _____

18. A cheese tray contains slices of Swiss cheese and cheddar cheese. If you randomly pick a slice of cheese, $P(\text{Swiss}) = 0.45$. Find $P(\text{cheddar})$. If there are 200 slices of cheese, how many slices of Swiss cheese are on the tray? _____

19. For a raffle 10,000 tickets are sold. One ticket is drawn at random to determine a winner. Find the probability and odds of winning. _____

Practice 11-5 Independent and Dependent Events

A bag contains 3 black and 2 white marbles. A marble is drawn at random and then replaced. Find each probability.

1. P(2 blacks) _____

2. P(black, white) _____

3. P(white, black) _____

4. P(2 whites) _____

Each letter from the word MISSISSIPPI is written on a separate slip of paper. The 11 slips of paper are placed in a sack and two slips are drawn at random. The first pick is not replaced.

5. Find the probability that the first letter is M and the second letter is I. _____

6. Find the probability that the first letter is I and the second letter is P. _____

7. Find the probability that the first letter is S and the second letter is also S. _____

Solve.

8. On a TV game show, you can win a car by drawing two aces from a standard deck of cards. The first card is not replaced. What is your probability of winning?

_____

9. You roll a number cube eight times, and each time you roll a 4. What is the probability that on the ninth roll, you will roll a 6?

_____

10. Two letters of the alphabet are chosen randomly without replacement. Find each probability.

a. P(both vowels) _____

b. P(both consonants) _____

11. There are 4 brown shoes and 10 black shoes on the floor. Your puppy carries away two shoes and puts one shoe in the trash can and one shoe in the laundry basket.

a. Complete the tree diagram to show the probability of each outcome.

trash		laundry
	brown <	brown
		black
<		
	black <	brown
		black

b. What is the probability that there will be a brown shoe in both the trash and the laundry basket? _____

12. Use the data at the right to find P(right-handed male) and P(left-handed female) if one person is chosen at random.

_____

	Male	Female
Right-handed	86	83
Left-handed	14	17
Total	100	100

Practice 11-6 Problem-Solving Strategy: Simulate the Problem

Solve by simulating the problem. Show all your work.

You and your partner play a game in which you each toss a coin. You score a point for each head and your partner scores a point for each tail. The first person to score ten points wins.

1. **a.** The score is 7 to 9 in favor of your partner when you must stop. If you continue the game later, what is the probability that you will win? Hint: Think of how many turns the game may last. _____

    b. What is the probability that your partner will win? _____

2. **a.** The score is 7 to 8 in your favor when you must stop. If you continue the game later, what is the probability that you will win? Hint: Think of how many turns the game may last.

    _____

    b. What is the probability that your partner will win? _____

A weather forecaster reports that the probability for sunny weather each day for the next few days is 50%. You begin a three-day camping trip.

3. Simulate the situation to find the probability of three sunny days in a row.

    _____

4. Simulate the situation to find the probability of only two sunny days out of the three.

    _____

5. Simulate the situation to find the probability of only one sunny day out of the three.

    _____

6. Simulate the situation to find the probability of no sun for any of the three days.

    _____

A basketball player scores a basket on about 1 out of every 6 shots.

7. Explain how you could use a number cube to simulate the player's shooting average.

    _____

8. Use your simulation to find the probability of the player making 4 out of 5 of her next shots. _____

Practice 11-7 Analyzing Games and Making Predictions

For each game, the winner is the player with the most points after 20 rounds. Decide whether each game is fair.

1. Two number cubes are rolled. Player A subtracts the smaller number from the larger number, Player B divides the smaller by the larger; the smaller result wins a point.

   _____

2. Two number cubes are rolled. Player A adds the two numbers and then multiplies by 2. Player B multiplies the first number by 3 and then adds the second number. The larger result wins a point.

   _____

3. Two number cubes are rolled. The numbers are added. If the sum is even, Player A wins a point. If the sum is odd, Player B wins a point.

   _____

4. Two number cubes are rolled. If the product is odd, Player A wins a point. If the product is even, Player B wins a point.

   _____

Use these random digits in Exercises 5–10.

| 23948 | 71477 | 12573 | 05954 | 65628 |
| 22310 | 09311 | 94864 | 41261 | 09943 |

5. Jason guesses on a multiple-choice test. There are 50 questions, each with 5 possible answers. What digits could you use for a correct guess? What digits could you use for an incorrect guess?

   _____

6. Based on your answer for Exercise 5 and using the random digits, what will Jason's score be?

   _____

   _____

7. If the probability that Julie guesses correctly is 50%, what digits could you use for a correct guess and for an incorrect guess?

   _____

8. Based on your answer for Exercise 7 and using the random digits, what will Julie's score be?

   _____

   _____

9. The probability that Aaron guesses correctly is 80%. What digits could you use for a correct guess and an incorrect guess for Aaron?

   _____

10. Based on your answer for Exercise 9, and using the random digits, what will Aaron's score be?

   _____

   _____

Practice 11-8 Making Decisions with Probability

Find each answer.

1. A bakery inspects a sample of 800 pastries and finds that 12 are defective. Based on these data, what is the probability that a pastry is defective?

   _____

2. After altering some machinery, the bakery inspects a new sample of 1,500 pastries and finds that 16 are defective. Did quality improve? Explain.

   _____

   _____

Refer to the chart for Exercises 3–6.

Process Control Chart for Defective Pastry

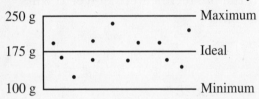

3. What is the ideal weight of a pastry?

   _____

4. What are the maximum and minimum acceptable weights of a pastry?

   _____

5. What is the range of acceptable values?

   _____

6. What does the range tell you?

   _____

   _____

Make a prediction.

7. A car rental agency rented 343 cars last week. Out of those cars, 3 were returned because of mechanical problems. Predict how many cars will be returned for mechanical problems out of 10,000 rentals.

   _____

8. A roller bearing manufacturer found 4 defective roller bearings out of a sample of 500 bearings. Based on this sample, predict how many defective bearings could be expected out of 1,000,000 bearings.

   _____

Enrichment: Minds on Math

For Lessons 1-1 through 1-3

1-1

How can you write four 5s to represent 56?

1-2

Which 8 sides of the small squares would you remove to leave 2 squares?

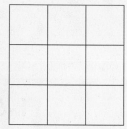

1-3

What whole number increased by the sum of its digits equals 94?

◼️◼️ Enrichment: Minds on Math

For Lessons 1-4 through 1-7

1-4

I am a two-digit multiple of 6. The sum of my digits is 4 greater than their difference. If you reverse my digits, the number formed is smaller than I am and is also a multiple of 6. What number am I?

1-5

What is the least four-digit number that has 2, 3, 5, and 7 as factors?

1-6

If 3 cooks can make 15 pizzas in $1\frac{1}{2}$ hours, how long does it take 6 cooks to make 20 pizzas?

1-7

Rita and Roberta are trying to decide when they will both have the same day off so they can go shopping together. Rita is off every seventh day and Roberta is off every eighth day. Rita is off today and Roberta is off tomorrow. How many days will it be before they will both have the same day off?

Enrichment: Minds on Math

For Lessons 1-8 through 1-11

1-8

A number that reads the same backwards as forwards is called a palindrome. There are 90 three-digit palindromes and 90 four-digit palindromes. How many five-digit palindromes are there?

1-9

Geri has a grandfather clock that chimes once on each half hour and the number of the hour on each hour. How many times does her clock chime in a 24-hour period?

1-10

Albert has a 3-gallon bucket and a 5-gallon bucket. How can he use these buckets to get exactly 4 gallons of water into one of the buckets?

1-11

Ice hockey, football, basketball, and golf are the favorite sports of Shelby, Ashley, Gary, and Greg. Gary does not like ice hockey or football. Shelby's favorite sport is not played with a ball. Greg's favorite is not basketball or golf and Ashley does not like a sport that uses a stick or a club. What sport does each person like best?

■■■■■ *Enrichment: Minds on Math*   *For Lessons 2-1 through 2-3*

2-1

A data set contains five numbers. Adding a 5
to the data set decreases the mean by 5.
What is the mean of the original data set?

2-2

Suppose one person tells a story to four people in 20
minutes. Then each of those people tell the story to four
other people in 20 minutes. How long will it be before
1.25 million people have heard the story?

2-3

Melissa harvested 5 quarts of strawberries from her
strawberry patch the first year she planted it. This year
she harvested 320 quarts. If her harvest doubles each
year, when did she harvest 80 quarts?

▬▬ *Enrichment: Minds on Math* *For Lessons 2-4 through 2-7*

2-4

Martha has four more sisters than brothers. How many more sisters than brothers does her brother Jarod have?

2-5

We are two positive integers whose product is 24,999,999 and whose positive difference is as small as possible. What integers are we?

2-6

In 10 seconds a blade of a ceiling fan moves through 60 right angles. How many complete revolutions does the blade make in a minute?

2-7

Write 100 using five 5s.

▬▬▬ *Enrichment: Minds on Math* *For Lessons 2-8 through 2-11*

2-8

Two planes depart from the same airport at the same time in opposite directions. One of the planes travels 60 miles per hour faster than the other plane. They are 1,820 miles apart after 2 hours. How fast is each plane traveling?

2-9

Wesley has 3 different cards that he has placed side-by-side on a table. Each card is either blue, red, or green and contains the number 1, 2, or 3. The blue card is to the left of the red card, which is not a 1 or a 2. The green card is to the right of the blue card, which is a 2. Card 1 is to the left of card 3. What is the order of the cards?

2-10

Becki thinks of a number. If she multiplies her number by 8, adds 10, and then divides by 5, the result is 26. What is Becki's number?

2-11

Martina went shopping. She spent a fifth of what she had in her wallet and then a fifth of what remained. In all she spent $36. How much did she start with?

Enrichment: Minds on Math

3-1

How many numbers from 0 to 1,000 have digits that have a sum of 10?

3-2

On a recent airline flight there was 1 empty seat for every 3 passengers. If there were 132 seats available, how many passengers were on the flight?

3-3

Look for a pattern in the equations below. Then find the value of 75^2, 85^2, and 95^2.

$15^2 =$ 225
$25^2 =$ 625
$35^2 = 1,225$
$45^2 = 2,025$
$55^2 = 3,025$
$65^2 = 4,225$

▄▄▄▄ *Enrichment: Minds on Math*   *For Lessons 3-4 through 3-6*

3-4

Les, Quinn, Shari, and Nate shared a box of pencils equally. Quinn then shared all of the pencils he got equally with 5 other friends. If Quinn and each of his friends got 3 pencils, how many pencils were in the box?

3-5

Which positive one-digit numbers do * and # stand for in the expressions below?

$$\frac{* + \#}{* - \#} = 1\frac{1}{2}$$

3-6

Derrick is thinking of a negative integer. When he multiplies the integer by itself and then adds three times the integer to the product, he gets 180. What is Derrick's integer?

▰▰ *Enrichment: Minds on Math* **For Lessons 3-7 through 3-10**

3-7

Tim has more than 50 marbles but less than 100 marbles. He gets a remainder of 6 when he divides the number of marbles by either 8 or 9. How many marbles does Tim have?

3-8

Write the numbers 1 through 7 in the circles so that the numbers in each line of connected circles total 12.

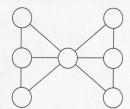

3-9

Look for a pattern in the equations below. Then find the value of $199^2 - 198^2$ and $2,150^2 - 2,149^2$.

$1^2 - 0^2 = 1$
$2^2 - 1^2 = 3$
$3^2 - 2^2 = 5$
$4^2 - 3^2 = 7$
$5^2 - 4^2 = 9$

3-10

Change the operation in one place in the expression below to make the value 100.

$1 + 2 + 3 + 4 + 5 + 6 + 7 + 8 + 9$

■■■■■*Enrichment: Minds on Math* *For Lessons 4-1 through 4-3*

4-1

I am a 4-digit number that is the same when my digits are written backwards. The sum of my outside digits is 6 times the sum of my two middle digits. What number am I?

4-2

Valeska told Ken that she has invented a new operation that uses the symbol *. She told him that $x * y$ means $2x - y$. Ken then evaluated $10 * 9$ and $10 * 10$, and said that $10 * 10$ has the greater value. Is Ken correct? Justify your answer.

4-3

Wesley said that he can use each of the numbers 1, 2, 3, and 4 exactly once and the operations of addition and multiplication to write an expression with a value of 15. Show that Wesley's statement is correct.

Enrichment: Minds on Math

For Lessons 4-4 through 4-6

4-4

The ratio of blue marbles to green marbles in a bag is 2 to 5. There are 25 green marbles. What is the smallest number of marbles and which color would you have to add to the bag so that the ratio of blue to green is 1 to 3?

4-5

A cat weighs 10 pounds plus half its weight. How much does the cat weigh?

4-6

Hannah gave Jane as many books as Jane had already. When Jane received these books, she asked Hannah how many books she had left. Jane then gave this number of books back to Hannah. Hannah then gave Jane back as many books as Jane had left. This left Hannah without any books and left Jane with 80 books. How many books did Hannah and Jane have to begin with?

Enrichment: Minds on Math   *For Lessons 4-7 through 4-10*

4-7

January 1, 1901 was on a Tuesday. What day of the week will January 1, 2001 be on?

4-8

In a survey of 100 students at Holland School, 70 said they liked vanilla yogurt, 60 said they liked peach yogurt, and 50 said they liked both. How many of the students surveyed did not say they liked either flavor?

4-9

The last three digits of Allison's license plate have a product of 360. The sum of the digits is 22 and the digits are in order from the least to the greatest. What are the last three digits of her license plate?

4-10

Frances wants to build a fence to make a square dog pen. She wants each side of the dog pen to measure 25 feet and she will place a fence post every 5 feet. How many fence posts will Frances need?

Enrichment: Minds on Math

5-1

A machine at a local factory has 3 gears. One gear must be replaced every 3 months, another every 5 months, and the third every 6 months. All of the gears were just replaced. How long will it be before all 3 gears will need to be replaced at the same time again?

5-2

The image of point A after
 the translation $(x, y) \rightarrow (x + 4, y - 10)$,
 a reflection over the x-axis,
 a rotation of 180° about the origin,
 a reflection over the y-axis, and
 the translation $(x, y) \rightarrow (x - 2, y + 5)$
is $A'(0, 0)$. What are the coordinates of point A?

5-3

There were 11 days of rain one month in Boston. Of the remaining days, two-fifths were sunny, one-fourth were cloudy, and it snowed on the other 7 days. How many days were in the month?

Enrichment: Minds on Math
For Lessons 5-4 through 5-6

5-4

Use eight 8s to form an addition expression with value 1,000.

5-5

Dee, Sara, and Tyrone ordered a pizza to share. The cost of the pizza was $10. Sara ate less than everyone else, so Dee and Tyrone decided that she did not have to pay the same as they did for the pizza. They decided to have Sara pay half of what they paid. What did Sara pay for the pizza?

5-6

I am the slope-intercept form of a linear equation. My slope is $\frac{1}{2}$ of my y-intercept. The coordinates of one of the points on my line is (1, 1). What is my slope?

Enrichment: Minds on Math *For Lessons 5-7 through 5-10*

5-7

Bob got on an elevator. He rode up 7 floors, down 5 floors, up 3 floors, up 1 floor, and then down 2 floors. He got off the elevator at the eighth floor. On what floor did he start?

5-8

Mr. Thomas has a lot shaped like the drawing at right. He wants to divide it so that each of his 4 children get a lot that is exactly the same size and shape as the others. How can he do this?

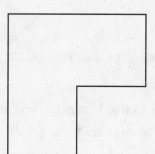

5-9

Mrs. Ramon and her two children want to cross the river in a boat that can safely hold 160 lb of weight at any one time. Mrs. Ramon weighs 120 lb and her children each weigh 80 lb. How can they all cross the river?

5-10

The average score in five basketball games was 67. The first four scores were 74, 61, 83, and 52. What was the score for the fifth game?

Enrichment: Minds on Math

6-1

Jake found an interesting five-digit number. He noticed that when he put a 1 after it, the new number was 3 times as large as the number formed by putting a 1 before it. What was Jake's number?

6-2

If it took Gary 1 minute to fill his aquarium $\frac{1}{3}$ full, how long will it take him to fill it $\frac{3}{4}$ full?

6-3

Find the missing numbers in the sequence below if each term after the first two is the sum of the two preceding terms.

7, ___, ___, ___, ___, 11

■■■■ Enrichment: Minds on Math

For Lessons 6-4 through 6-6

6-4

I am the largest four-digit number with exactly 3 factors that are positive integers. What number am I?

6-5

Which 5 sides of the small squares would you remove to leave 3 small congruent squares?

6-6

What is the next term in the sequence below?

1, 7, 25, 61, 121, . . .

Enrichment: Minds on Math

6-7

At the track meet, one student told another that one-sixth of the people running on the race track were in front of Jesse and three-fourths were behind her. How many people were in the race?

6-8

There are 1,200 students at Thomas Alternative School. Each student takes 5 classes a day and each teacher teaches 4 classes. If each class has 30 students and 1 teacher, how many teachers does the school have?

6-9

I am a two-digit prime number. The difference of my digits is 4 and their product is 21. I am greater than 50. What number am I?

6-10

I am a three-digit number. My square root is a perfect square. The square root of my square root is also a perfect square. What number am I?

▰▰▰▰ *Enrichment: Minds on Math*   *For Lessons 7-1 through 7-3*

7-1

One month, Meredith's parents doubled her monthly allowance. The next month, they increased her allowance by $3. The next month, they cut her allowance in half. Is her allowance more or less now than her original allowance? By how much?

7-2

If every seven-digit whole number is a possible telephone number except those that begin with 0 or 1, what fraction of telephone numbers begins with 9 and ends with 0?

7-3

Dan and Alex ran a 50-m race. When Dan crossed the finish line, Alex was 10 m behind him. If they both run at their original rates and Dan starts 10 m behind the start line in a second race, what will happen?

■■■ *Enrichment: Minds on Math* *For Lessons 7-4 through 7-6*

7-4

Find the minimum number of moves to exchange places of the black and white chips. The chips can move one space at a time vertically, horizontally, or diagonally. Only one chip can occupy a square.

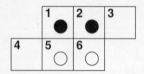

7-5

A total of 120 five-digit numbers can be formed using each of the digits 1, 2, 3, 4, and 5. The beginning of the list of these numbers arranged from least to greatest is shown below. If you continue this list up to 54,321, what number is the 75th number listed?

12,345   12,354   12,435   12,453

7-6

How many ways can you arrange the letters A, B, C, and D in a row if A and B are never next to each other?

▄▄▄ *Enrichment: Minds on Math*   *For Lessons 7-7 through 7-9*

7-7

Wilma can row downstream at 10 miles per hour
and upstream at 6 miles per hour. What is the rate
of the current?

7-8

Eighteen people are sitting in chairs that are equally spaced
around a round table. The chairs are numbered 1 to 18.
What is the number of the chair of the person directly
across from the person whose chair number is 6?'

7-9

The mean of x, 3, $4x - 3$, $x + 4$, -16, 9, and $x - 4$ is 2.
What is the median?

▄▄▄▄▄ *Enrichment: Minds on Math*   *For Lessons 8-1 through 8-3*

8-1

I am a proper fraction in lowest terms. My two-digit numerator is a multiple of 7 and my two-digit denominator is a multiple of 8. The sum of the digits of my numerator is 3 greater than the sum of the digits of my denominator. What fraction am I?

8-2

Kira, Irene, and Tim bought 24 CDs at a recent sale at the CD Warehouse. Kira bought 2 less than twice the number of CDs that Irene bought. Irene bought 2 more than half as many as Tim. How many CDs did each person buy?

8-3

Write a number using three 3s that equals 4.

Enrichment: Minds on Math

8-4

One number is 5 less than another number. The ratio of the first number to the second number is 5 to 6. What are the two numbers?

8-5

Mr. and Mrs. Ramirez have 4 sons and each son has 1 sister. How many people are in the Ramirez family?

8-6

How does the area of a small triangle compare to the area of the large triangle?

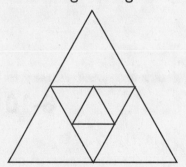

Enrichment: Minds on Math
For Lessons 8-7 through 8-10

8-7

Each edge of a cube is increased by 50%. What is the percent of increase of the surface area of the cube?

8-8

I am a four-digit perfect square. The number formed by my last two digits is my square root. What number am I?

8-9

I am an acute angle in a right triangle. My tangent ratio is $\frac{3}{4}$. What is my sine ratio?

8-10

How many different lines can you draw to connect 6 points, no 3 of which lie on the same line?

Enrichment: Minds on Math   *For Lessons 9-1 through 9-3*

9-1

Divide the square shown into 4 congruent pieces so that each piece contains 3 of the circles.

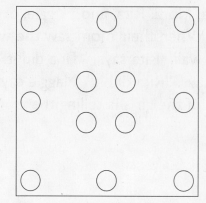

9-2

In a certain litter of puppies two puppies could see out of the right eye, three could see out of the left eye, exactly five could not see out of the right eye, and exactly four could not see out of the left eye. What is the least number of puppies in the litter?

9-3

Consider the expression below. Find the digit in the hundreds place in the sum.

$$7 + 77 + 777 + \ldots + 77{,}777{,}777{,}777{,}777{,}777{,}777{,}777$$

▰▰▰ Enrichment: Minds on Math   *For Lessons 9-4 through 9-6*

9-4

One of four sisters, Tina, Nora, Rita, and Maggie, drew on the wall of their room. When their mom saw the wall, she asked who drew on the wall. Rita says, "Tina did it." Nora says, "Rita did it." Tina says, "Rita did it." Maggie says, "I didn't do it." If only one of the girls is telling the truth, who did it?

9-5

Ardell selects a three-digit number at random from all three-digit numbers 100 through 999. What is the probability that the number Ardell selected is a perfect square?

9-6

There are 12 teams in a basketball league. The league is divided into two divisions. There are 6 teams in each division. Each team must play each team in its division twice and each team in the other division once during a season. What is the total number of league games each year?

Enrichment: Minds on Math *For Lessons 9-7 through 9-10*

9-7

Frank is between Fran and Ann. Fran is 100 feet from Frank and Frank is 300 feet from Ann. They all walk at constant speeds and in the same direction. In 6 minutes Fran passes Frank. In another 6 minutes Fran passes Ann. How many minutes did it take Frank to pass Ann?

9-8

Ten consecutive integers greater than 5 billion are each raised to the fifth power. The powers are then added together. What is the ones digit of the sum?

9-9

In how many ways can 47 be written as the sum of two prime numbers?

9-10

The areas of three faces of a rectangular prism are 48 cm^2, 54 cm^2, and 72 cm^2. What are the lengths of the edges?

▰▰▰*Enrichment: Minds on Math*   *For Lessons 10-1 through 10-3*

10-1

Jamil bought half as many carnival tickets as Wanda. If Wanda buys 12 more tickets, Jamil will have $\frac{2}{5}$ the number of tickets that Wanda has. How many tickets did Jamil buy?

10-2

Draw a net for a cube that has at most three squares in a line. Then write the letters C, U, B, and E in four squares of your net so that when the net is folded, the word "CUBE" wraps around the cube.

10-3

Keith baked muffins and gave $\frac{3}{4}$ of them to Peter. Peter then gave away a dozen of the muffins. Peter ended up with 6 muffins. How many muffins did Keith bake?

▰▰▰ *Enrichment: Minds on Math* *For Lessons 10-4 through 10-7*

10-4

In Mr. Bowman's class, 80% of the students eat lunch at school. Of those students, 25% bring their lunch. Of those students, 20% buy their drink. What percent of the total number of students in Mr. Bowman's class bring their lunch and buy their drink?

10-5

Loni's teacher took a survey of the pets owned by students in the class. Fifteen students had dogs, 14 had cats, and 7 had birds. None of the students had both cats and birds, 8 had dogs and cats, and 3 had dogs and birds. How many students in the class had only dogs?

10-6

A bird can fly $\frac{1}{4}$ mile in $\frac{1}{2}$ minute. How far can the bird fly in 5 minutes?

10-7

A pyramid has 10 edges. How many triangular faces does this pyramid have?

Enrichment: Minds on Math *For Lessons 10-8 through 10-11*

10-8

I am a percent that is greater than 100%. The sum of my three digits is 7. I can be written as a two-digit decimal that is less than 2. What percent am I?

10-9

What fraction in simplest form is $\frac{4}{9}$ of its reciprocal?

10-10

Gil threw 4 darts at a target composed of 2 sections, A and B. One of Gil's darts landed in A and 3 landed in B. His score was 29. Then Ellen threw 3 darts and 1 landed in A and 2 landed in B. Her score was 23. How many points are A and B worth?

10-11

It takes 4 hours to fill a swimming pool with the drain closed. It takes 5 hours to drain the same pool. When Joey began to fill the pool, he accidently left the drain open. How long did it take before the pool was full?

▰▰▰ Enrichment: Minds on Math *For Lessons 11-1 through 11-3*

11-1

Identical cubes are stacked in the corner of a
store as shown. How many of the
cubes cannot be seen?

11-2

Suppose you make $1,000 every time the hands of a clock
form a right angle. How much money would you make in
24 hours?

11-3

Two numbers are picked from 3, 4, 5, 6, and 7 without
being replaced. What is the probability that the product
of the two numbers is a multiple of 4?

Enrichment: Minds on Math   *For Lessons 11-4 through 11-6*

11-4

Two rectangles have perimeters of 144 cm. What is the greatest possible difference between their areas if the length and the width of both rectangles are integers?

11-5

Two ants race around the perimeter of a unit square. They both start at the same vertex and move clockwise. One ant runs at the constant rate of 1 unit per second. The other ant runs at the constant rate of 2 units per second. How far apart will they be after 17 seconds?

11-6

What is the greatest number of boxes with dimensions $2 \times 2 \times 3$ that can be placed inside a box with dimensions $3 \times 4 \times 5$?

Enrichment: Minds on Math   *For Lessons 11-7 through 11-8*

11-7

A line has nonzero slope equal to twice the *x*-intercept and half the *y*-intercept. What is its equation in slope-intercept form?

11-8

The edges of a cube are 10 cm long. A fly lands on a vertex of the cube and then walks along just the edges. What is the greatest distance the fly could walk to reach the vertex a second time and without retracing an edge?